"*No Ordinary Marriage* is an extraordinary book. What makes this work stand out in an overcrowded marketplace of 'how to' books is its compelling vision of marriage for the glory of God. I know of few books on marriage that combine elegant writing, sound doctrine, clear illustrations, and practical advice in equal measure. This is a book on marriage made in heaven. No one, or couple, who reads this book will look at marriage in an ordinary way again."

Kevin J. Vanhoozer, Research Professor of Systematic Theology, Trinity Evangelical Divinity School

"This is no ordinary book on marriage. Dr. Tim Savage clears away the rubble and shows you the treasure that can make any marriage rich: a life lived for the glory of God. Embrace the message of this book and it will transform your marriage, your family, and your entire life."

Colin S. Smith, Senior Pastor, The Orchard Evangelical Free Church; Bible Teacher, Unlocking the Bible

"Being a speaker and writer on marriage, I have read dozens of books on marriage, and *No Ordinary Marriage* is by far the best. Dr. Tim Savage moves his readers beyond a marriage manual of do's and don'ts into the realm of 'being' in a union for the glory of God—producing a unity that is beyond earthly description. A must read for one and all."

Naomi Rhode, Certified Speaking Professional; Former President, National Speakers Association; recipient, Council of Peers Award for Excellence, Speaker Hall of Fame; author, *The Gift of Family*

"*No Ordinary Marriage* explains how a marriage is intended to glorify God. Dr. Tim Savage writes not in a spirit of condemnation, but rather of encouragement as he paints a picture of what marriage is really meant to be. In reading this book, Sheryl—my wife of nearly 36 years—and I found ourselves challenged and inspired to rely on God as the core of our marriage."

Alice Cooper, rock star

D0167897

no ordinary
MARRIAGE

no ordinary

MARRIAGE

TOGETHER FOR GOD'S GLORY

TIM
SAVAGE

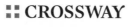

WHEATON, ILLINOIS

Trade paperback ISBN:978-1-4335-3033-3

PDF ISBN: 978-1-4335-3034-0

Mobipocket ISBN: 978-1-4335-3035-7

ePub ISBN: 978-1-4335-3036-4

Library of Congress Cataloging-in-Publication Data
    Savage, Timothy B.
    No ordinary marriage : together for God's glory / Tim
      Savage.
      p. cm.
    Includes bibliographical references and indexes.
    ISBN 978-1-4335-3033-3 (tp)
    1. Marriage—Religious aspects—Christianity. I. Title.
BV835.S28 2012
248.8'44—dc23   2011049820

Crossway is a publishing ministry of Good News Publishers.

VP		21	20	19	18	17	16	15	14	13	12
14	13	12	11	10	9	8	7	6	5	4	3	2	1

Lesli

CONTENTS

PROLOGUE

It would be difficult to overestimate the beauty of marriage. Right from the start, marriage was depicted in terms almost too sublime for human comprehension— "and the two shall become one flesh." Here is a union of perfect harmony, where intimacy and companionship are interwoven into a thrilling cohesion. Two people swept up in a torrent of mutual affection—what could be more exhilarating than marriage?

But marriage has lost some of its luster. Today only half the people eligible for marriage actually tie the knot,[1] and many who do marry discover the knot loosely fastened, binding them just long enough to meet, mate, and bear a child. After that—as one Ivy League study puts it—there is "no evolutionary need for the beating heart and sweaty palms associated with the high point of passion."[2] Too seldom do romantic sparks fan into lasting flames.

This is disappointing, but disappointment can be a good thing. It proves that, contrary to the minimalistic expectations of evolutionary biology, we possess a deep-seated conviction that marriage ought to deliver more: more intimacy, more satisfaction, more durability. And thankfully, there is more. The aim of this book is to discover just how much more—to peel back the veil on the most pivotal social institution of history and expose the multilayered beauty of the relationship we call marriage. There is vastly more to this union than meets the contemporary eye.

Many people have helped to open my eyes. Hank, Karen, and Joel Martin and Jerry and Joan Colangelo have opened the doors of their mountain and ocean retreats, respectively, providing inspiration for my writing. The gifted team at Crossway— Justin Taylor, Mattie Wolf, and Josh Dennis—have embraced this book with enthusiastic support. Steve Laube, my agent, has provided invaluable counsel. My mentors in marriage—Ted and Claudia Limpic, Fred and Ann Sewell, Harold and Gini Hoehner, Murray and Jennifer Harris, Bill and Peggy Eaton, and, for more than five decades, Bill and Betty Savage—have each in their unique ways expanded my horizons and provided stunning personal portraits of the beauty of the marital union. To these friends, positioned strategically along my path, I offer my deep and humble gratitude.

Finally, to the person who has, with a radiance undimmed by circumstance and an earnestness seasoned by laughter, favored me with the best of her love and encouraged me always to seek more in marriage—to Lesli, with whom I've shared every day of a very short thirty-two years, I offer the keys to my heart.

PART ONE

GLORY WITHOUT LIMITS

1

INTRODUCTION

A BINDING GLORY

What is more sweet than to live with her with whom you are united in body and soul, who talks with you in secret affection, to whom you have committed all your faith and your fortune? What in all nature is lovelier? Nothing is more safe, felicitous, tranquil, pleasant and lovable than marriage.

DESIDERIUS ERASMUS

For sheer joy, nothing compares to a wedding. The bride emerges at the top of the aisle accompanied by the strains of an exalted musical score, her face and form radiating an almost celestial beauty and her heart throbbing with a treasury of dreams coming true. Her counterpart, the groom, waits—waits for what seems an eternity!—for the processing angel to arrive at his side and for that cherished hand to be tucked under his arm by the guardian who has nurtured her so carefully and whose own storehouse of memories have, in the short space of thirty steps, come flooding back in a cataract of emotion. The congregation, sensing the ecstasy of the moment, rises spontaneously to its feet in a display of reverence befitting the arrival of a heavenly dignitary. The presiding official averts his eyes briefly from the sight of unrestrained love before him and seeks the composure to find words to frame a scene almost too sublime for human utterance. It is a moment of unparalleled joy.

There are too few such moments in life. In a world growing increasingly grim, we find little worth celebrating. A victory by a local sports team perhaps, a promotion to higher echelons of management, a diploma signifying the completion of a degree—these are the things we celebrate. And rightly so. But they are comparatively minor glories, fading quickly with the passage of time and causing us to pine for something more enduring, something able to nurture our souls at the deepest level.

FULFILLMENT IN MARRIAGE

Many seek deeper fulfillment in marriage. What could be more encouraging than the union of two people whose lives intermingle in a symphony of mutual support, whose destinies run together in a rainbow of shared dreams, whose vows cement an indissoluble bond of tenderness and compassion? Marriage! It may be the most celebrated event of human experience.

No wonder we revel in the wedding. It serves as a base camp from which lovers make an ascent on a peak so grand it takes a lifetime to discover its many wonders. It marks the beginning of a relationship which, more than perhaps any other in life, holds out promise of enduring happiness. From the moment of dramatic fusion on the honeymoon to the settled unity of confidants on the golden anniversary, the marital partnership will produce life's most satisfying moments.

But here we encounter a painful irony. The wedding, which is intended to inaugurate the first of many steps along the path of marital bliss, often represents the high point of the marriage relationship. Once the ceremony is over, rather than advance to higher slopes of marital contentment, couples frequently begin a slow and inexorable slide into disappointment and mediocrity.

We all know that one of the greatest social scourges of our day is the failure of marriages, and not just marriages that collapse in separation and divorce, but also those which, while remaining "intact," become severely strained and emotionally scarred. One recent study reveals that nine out of ten marriages are "filled with dissatisfaction in every dimension of the relationship."[1] Nor is this just a modern malady. Marital unhappiness has been a blemish on every age. Martin Luther, the great sixteenth-century Christian Reformer whose own marriage became a model for generations of German partnerships, commented on the absence of good marriages in his day: "When I see a husband and a wife who are at one, I am as glad as if I were in a garden of roses. It is rare."[2]

How can a union which begins so promisingly become mired in the quicksands of indifference and despair? It is enough to cause the cynical among us to ask whether marriage is just a cruel trick, luring us with the promise of golden peaks to be conquered but concealing the very real danger of breakup on the rocks below. It ought to give us pause. It ought to prompt us to evaluate soberly the very desirability of marriage. If matrimony is more likely to blight than to bless, ought not we to be extremely careful before embarking on such a union?

Remarkably, few show such restraint. Modern sociologists report that marriage—or the increasingly popular practice of cohabitation—is enjoying a resurgence in the popular mind. Even those who have good reason to mistrust marriage, those who have suffered the pangs of a failed first marriage or who have grown up in homes crippled by indifference or animosity between parents, still aspire "to tie the knot." How can this be, especially when experience ought to discourage such a union?

There can be only one answer. We are romantics at heart. We cling to the notion that marriage can be satisfying. We refuse to believe that the relationship between a man and a woman is bound to fail. We nurture the ideal, rooted deeply in our subconsciouses, that great rewards await couples who are in love.

THE PATH TO THE MARITAL SUMMIT

But what happens when the initial spark of romance begins to fade, when the unbridled joy of the wedding is insufficient to propel a husband and a wife to the heights of lasting love, when the shared experiences of intimate companionship, sexual union, and raising children fail to elevate two lovers to the summit of marital fulfillment—what then do we say to the couple whose lofty hopes seem to have peaked at the altar?

We say with great emphasis and unstinting confidence: "Your hopes of an enduring union are *not* futile!" "Your vision of marital fulfillment is *not* a deception!" "Your dreams of an increasingly intimate bond are *not* beyond the realm of possibility!" "Marriage *can* be rewarding!" But—and here is a crucial qualification—such lofty ideals are by no means automatically realized. Husbands and wives must exercise vigilance. They must be committed to work for this prize. In particular, they must cling tenaciously to the one piece of equipment that guarantees a safe ascent to the marital summit. They must fasten themselves to the rope that binds them together as one.

And what is that rope?

It is *the glory of God*!

When husbands and wives cling firmly to the lifeline of God's glory and do so with a resolve appropriate to the importance of their joint expedition, the unbridled optimism of the wedding will be confirmed a hundred times over by an upward ascent that surpasses even their loftiest expectations. Their marriage can become a living miracle—a relationship grounded on earth but filled with the glory of heaven!

The purpose of this book is to examine the nature of the divine glory, which can sustain a marriage. We will marvel at its multifaceted radiance and rejoice at the very down-to-earth assistance it affords husbands and wives. We will see how partners in marriage, when they resolve to march in lockstep with the glory of God, are rescued from pitfalls and hoisted to awe-inspiring heights.

May our hearts—the hearts of men and women in love—yearn for nothing less than the binding power of God's glory!

2

SOMETHING BEYOND
OURSELVES

In a mutual relationship between two human beings, we know
that it can be sustained only if both acknowledge something
that has authority over them and if each trusts the other to
acknowledge this.

LESSLIE NEWBIGIN

The British schoolteacher George Mallory was asked in 1923 what
compelled him to be the first person to attempt an ascent of Mount
Everest. He responded wryly: "Because it is there!"[1] While such a
quip may explain what motivated an adventurer to risk his life on
a subfreezing precipice of ice and stone, it will hardly do for the more
demanding ascent of marriage. A more weighty rationale, a
more transcendent vision, is required to lift husbands and wives to
the heights of marital fulfillment.

Yet when amorous partners are asked why they venture an expedition as harrowing as marriage, they frequently respond with breezy
clichés. "We are attracted to each other." "We share similar interests." "He understands me better than anyone else." "She makes me
a stronger person." In other words, they are drawn together by what
is there—a winsome combination of mutual attraction, shared interests, and reciprocal love. While each of these comforts may prove
useful in the assault on marital peaks, none of them—nor all of them
together—is sufficient to sustain an enterprise as complex as marriage. Something weightier, something beyond what the couple itself
brings to the relationship, must *be there*.

THE GLORY OF GOD IN MARRIAGE

What is the necessary ingredient? It is the glory of God. Nothing catapults husbands and wives to the upper reaches of matrimony like God's glory. Tethered to divine glory there is no limit to the heights married couples can climb.

With such an assurance, we would expect God's glory to be the most treasured ingredient of marriage. Most often, it is not. We treasure others things far more—rings, sex, babies. But this is because we understand divine glory only in part. We imagine it to be exceedingly brilliant, even blinding, causing our spines to tingle and our breath to be stolen away. Emanating directly from God himself, we suppose it to be matchlessly beautiful, utterly awe-inspiring, and somewhat terrifying. Beyond that, we find it difficult to quantify. For most of us, the glory of God remains an abstraction cloaked in a mystery.

Yet divine glory is more accessible than we might think. According to King Solomon, the whole earth is filled with God's glory (Ps. 72:19). That means everywhere we look, from the tiniest molecule to the largest ocean, we see evidence of God's glory. Woven into the fabric of every bird of paradise, every polished agate, every towering sequoia, every emerald lake, every microscopic atom, and, especially, every human being—woven into every visible component of the physical world is a breathtaking display of the glory of the One who fashioned those components. And not just the visible world, but also the invisible universe—or multiuniverse as astral physicists now name interstellar space. In the words of King David, "The heavens declare the glory of God" (Ps. 19:1).

No wonder, in the opening pages of the Holy Scriptures, the work of creation receives unqualified affirmation. "God saw that it was good" (Gen. 1:4, 10, 12, 18, 21, 25). "God saw . . . it was *very good*" (Gen. 1:31). To the eyes of the Maker, whose mark of glory has been left on every cell in a billion galaxies, creation is exceptionally good—good because it trumpets, in its every dimension, the radiance of his glory. Creation, it seems, could not be better.

Shockingly, however, the eyes of the Creator detect a deficiency. "Then the LORD God said, 'It is *not good* that the man should be alone'" (Gen. 2:18). Anyone reading the first two chapters of Genesis is stunned by this negative assessment. After so many effusive affirmations, how could there possibly be a deficiency? The answer is that there remains one more step of creation, a step which will form the capstone of the Creator's handiwork and provide an even greater outburst of divine glory.

What is that step? It is to fashion the first marriage. In the words of the Lord himself: "I will make him a helper fit for him" (Gen. 2:18). In the union of man and woman, in the very first marriage, we find an unprecedented crescendo of divine glory.

To prepare the solitary man for a fresh infusion of glory, the Lord invites him into an open field to review a long procession of living creatures. The purpose of this zoological exercise is to identify whether any of the quadrupeds might correspond to him (Gen. 2:19–20). The exercise proves embarrassingly futile. None of the animals fits the bill—neither the porcupine nor the grasshopper, neither the duck nor the elephant. None is a suitable partner.

Made to feel his deficiency, the man is guided to the next step in the drama of unfolding glory—an operating room! Under sedation of divine anesthesia, he submits to the heavenly scalpel, and one of his ribs is extracted and fashioned into a perfect human counterpart (Gen. 2:21–22). Aroused from his slumber, he is presented with the work of the Surgeon's hand. It is a masterpiece so ravishingly suitable to him that he bursts into ecstatic praise: "This at last is bone of my bones and flesh of my flesh; she shall be called Woman, because she was taken out of Man" (Gen. 2:23).

The story of the first marriage never ceases to move us. Yet it is easy to miss its central point. The insight of these verses, an insight which ought to form the centerpiece of every marriage, is that there is more to matrimony than first meets the eye—in other words, more than what *is there*: more than mutual attraction, more than shared interests, and more than reciprocal love. There is *infinitely* more. There is the work of God, a work into which is woven more glory than all the glory of the prior works of creation—a glory brighter than that of the physical world below and the heavens above. In the first marriage, divine glory reaches a zenith.

MARRYING FOR GOD'S GLORY

The reason why there is so much glory in marriage is because there is so much of God in marriage. The biblical narrative is at pains to point out God's dynamic role in every step of the first union. First of all, God identifies a deficiency ("The LORD God said, 'It is not good that the man should be alone,'" Gen. 2:18). Secondly, he proposes a solution ("I will make him a helper fit for him," Gen. 2:18). Thirdly, he demonstrates a need ("The LORD God . . . brought [all the beasts] to the man to see what he would call them," Gen. 2:19–20). Fourthly, he executes a plan ("So the LORD God . . . took one of [the man's] ribs and . . . made . . . a woman," Gen. 2:21–22). And finally, he presents his handiwork ("The LORD God . . . brought her to the man," Gen. 2:22).

No other work of creation is reported in such detail. And its significance is not lost on the man: he breaks out into an impassioned song of thanksgiving, a robust lyric in honor not just of marriage but also of the One who, in fashioning it, has managed every detail to perfection.

We should do no less. We should, in our marriages, exult in the creative genius of the God who fashions our unions. But do we? Where are the voices ringing out the joyous refrain that marriage is, above everything else in creation, a work of incomparable glory? Such a tribute to God would strike a dissonant chord alongside the contemporary chorus that matrimony is essentially the work of two human beings, the simple achievement of consenting adults. Yet nothing could be further from the truth. If the Bible is to be believed— and we disbelieve it at our peril—marriage represents a high point of creation, a sparkling gem crafted by the Creator's hand, a union of unprecedented glory.

To ignore the glory of God in marriage is tantamount to pushing up a steep rock face without "the rope," which guarantees a safe ascent. It is to throw caution to the wind and to court inevitable disaster. Marriages are on firmest ground when partners are most focused on the glory of the Lord.

This is a crucial insight, and one underscored implicitly near the end of the second chapter of Genesis. "[For this cause], a man shall leave his father and his mother and [be united] to his wife," (v. 24). Naturally we want to ask, *For what cause* shall a man be united to his wife? The context supplies an answer: be-*cause* of everything God has done to form this union, be-*cause* of his involvement at every stage of its development, be-*cause* of the heavy allotment of glory he has invested in this partnership. We marry, not primarily for our own benefit and pleasure, nor principally for the comfort of mutual affection, nor ultimately for the joy of bearing and raising children—we marry be-*cause* in a work of unparalleled glory the Lord built this union. We marry be-*cause of his glory*.

So important is this one insight that we ought to put aside any prior notion of what produces a successful marriage and fasten exclusively onto this priceless truth. Here is the first principle of matrimony: we marry for the glory of God. When this becomes the guiding impulse of our unions, when the glory of God becomes our primary focus and greatest love, husbands and wives will track along a trajectory that is decidedly upward.

The amazing heights to which two people can ascend are hinted at in a tantalizing phrase at the end of Genesis 2: "They shall become one flesh" (v. 24). These five words announce one of the most dramatic realities of the Holy Scriptures, a reality as mysterious as it is breathtaking. Two individuals can be fused into one flesh. Extraordinary! The laws of physics seem to preclude it. But who would want it otherwise? What couple, buoyed by dreams of romantic love, would want anything less than to be bound together as one flesh?

We will explore the profound meaning and the thrilling implications of this term in a later chapter. Suffice it to observe now that the key to this mysterious oneness is God's glory. When two people resolve together to make the glory of God the energizing principle of their marriage, they become united in an increasingly seamless union. Nothing cements a marriage like focusing on the glory of the Lord. It is the tie that binds!

THE BINDING POWER OF GLORY

The binding properties of God's glory are simple in theory. Living organisms often need an external stimulus in order to fuse into a dynamic union. In the case of large organisms like nations, external forces become unifying agents, such as in the early days of the American Republic. It was the presence of a foreign adversary that prompted the patriot Thomas Paine to plead for the unification of thirteen loosely affiliated colonies. With quill in hand, he dramatized the terrors of the British menace in a propagandist pamphlet called *Common Sense* and issued the famous call to stand united against the opposition. Five hundred thousand copies of the booklet sold in the first year—an astonishing feat in a land of only two-and-a-half million people—and within ninety days the Continental Congress was formed, the Declaration of Independence was drafted, and a national army was conscripted. The presence of an external foe galvanized thirteen disparate colonies into *united* states.

Marriages, too, need a galvanizing agent, something external to what the partners themselves bring to the relationship. Sometimes a common adversary will do—financial difficulty or persistent illness can rally husbands and wives to form a united front. So can positive stimuli like raising children or planning for retirement. But none of these challenges can supply more than temporary cohesion. When financial burdens ease or children leave home, what then unifies marriage? The marital bond requires something more enduring, something bigger, something stronger.

Only one thing qualifies: the glory of God. Here is something so powerful that it transcends the most difficult challenges of life. Here is a provision so dependable that it can lift marriages to awe-inspiring heights. Here is a beacon so intense that it can show the way out of the darkest crisis. Here is a vision so permanent that it can outlast every temporary obstacle. Here is something supernatural, something beyond what mere humans bring to a partnership. Here is the cement of marriage. Here is the rope that binds. When husbands and wives unite for the glory of God, they unite indeed.

Surmounting Circumstances

The blessings of a union cemented by God's glory are manifold. First of all, such a marriage will be invulnerable to the vacillating circumstances of life. For many couples, change threatens marital harmony. When time steals away the youthful features of a wife or produces hormonal swings and unpredictable emotions, husbands may be tempted to look elsewhere for more attractive and predictable companionship. When the stresses of work erode a husband's self-respect and diminish his capacity for sensitivity, a wife may be tempted to look further afield for her encouragement.

But this will be the case only if partners focus on the oscillating drama of feminine beauty and masculine strength. If, instead, they cling to the glory of God as the rope that secures their union, the fluctuating circumstances of life will, far from destabilize their marriage, provide grounds for a deeper bond. This is because the glory of God is stronger in its capacity to bind than circumstances are in their capacity to divide.

Overcoming Differences

Secondly, when spouses fix their gazes on the glory of the Lord, they need never despair over apparent incompatibilities. While it is always important before marriage to assess the compatibility of a potential partner, the matter becomes moot after marriage. No alleged incompatibility will ever be able to break apart a husband and a wife who focus on the glory of God. Differences are incvitable in marriage: one partner may be quiet and deliberate and the other excitable and spontaneous; one may prefer directness and the other withdrawal. But such differences will never become "irreconcilable," a line of thinking too convenient for husbands and wives today. Even the most disparate partners will be unified by the glory of the Lord, because divine glory is more able to bind than incompatibilities are to divide.

Resisting Division

Thirdly, when two people are bound together by the glory of God, their marriage will become increasingly united over time. It is a sad feature of many contemporary partnerships that the opposite seems to occur: people grow apart. There is a presumption that, as the years pass, partners will inevitably grow weary of each other and be pushed in opposite directions by diverging interests. The perception, while often self-fulfilling, is unfortunate. When two people take aim at the glory of God, they are consumed by something so big that it creates synergy between them, causing them to climb enthusiastically to new and more exciting vistas. They will grow together spiritually, and when two people grow together spiritually they *never* weary of each other.

A very short thirty-two years ago a beautiful young bride and a somewhat overwhelmed groom stood before family and friends and recited their sacred wedding vows. They were perfectly matched and yet—at least in the mind of the overly pensive groom—they were very different from each other. They were deeply in love, but the husband-to-be wondered whether one day they would awaken to discover that their differences were driving them apart. What if they tired of each other? What then?

The young groom did not realize that his worries were completely allayed by the words he had secretly instructed the jeweler to inscribe inside the wedding band of his bride, the very words which, remarkably and unbeknownst to him, his bride had instructed her jeweler to etch inside the ring she presented to him. Later that evening, when at last alone, the newlyweds made the startling discovery. Written inside both rings was the identical prayer: "Together for God's glory!"

For more than three decades they have sought, often imperfectly and always in need of grace from above, to uphold the sacred words encircling their fourth fingers. Today they can testify to the blessing of ever-increasing oneness, in which new challenges are welcomed as opportunities to grow closer together and in which the spiritual adventures of each partner have become a source of endless fascination to the other. Now their bond is so deep that it cannot be captured in words but only cherished in the unspoken thoughts of their hearts. I know because those thoughts are my own, and the thoughts of that beautiful bride belong to Lesli, the woman I married!

Unity in marriage is simple conceptually. Only one thing is necessary: a mutual commitment to the Lord and his glory. Why, then, is it so difficult in practice? Why do contemporary marriages fail at an alarming rate? And why do so many of the marriages that remain intact become so dissatisfying?

THE TRIALS OF CONTEMPORARY MARRIAGES

The plight of matrimony in the West ought to provoke serious soul-searching. The pollster George Gallup Jr. has issued a sobering wake-up call: "[When] a disease . . . afflicts the majority of a populace, spreading pain and dysfunction throughout all age groups, we [naturally search] . . . for solutions. Yet [one] particular scourge has become so endemic that it is virtually ignored. The scourge is divorce, an oddly neglected topic in a nation that has the worst record of broken marriages in the entire world."[2]

Does our neglect of this epidemic suggest a resignation to defeat? Is marital discord an unavoidable feature of modern life? Perhaps it is—but perhaps not. There is certainly no abatement in the stream of literature designed to improve marriages. Consider the abundance of counsel flowing from national presses and Internet sites, advice for almost every conceivable eventuality in marriage, from how to land a partner through artful discourse to how to please a mate in bed. The sheer volume of blogs, seminars, magazines, CDs, DVDs, talk shows, radio programs, television interviews, and Internet banter committed specifically to enhancing marriage suggests that there remains an army of loyalists who believe matrimony is capable of being salvaged.

But—and here is the startling irony—despite all the optimism, marriages still languish. Is it possible that the stream of marital information is missing the mark? Are we packaging marital advice too lightly, ready for instant consumption, filled with creative techniques and clever applications, but avoiding the more difficult task of nurturing unions at the deeper level of hearts?

A review of the literature does reveal an approach that relies heavily on personal anecdotes, practical tips, and heart-tugging stories. Husbands and wives are given practical instruction—often in the form of entertaining vignettes—on what to do, when to do it, how to do it, and where to do it. Hopefully, such advice will strengthen their marriages. But evidence suggests something different. While how-to approaches may mesh well with an age eager to find solutions in practical steps, it is difficult to see how a relationship as substantial as the union of a man and a woman can be strengthened by advice parceled out in bite-sized morsels. Such superficiality will only exacerbate the problem. It trivializes marriage.

PERSPECTIVE BEFORE PRACTICE

We must recover the kernel of wisdom enshrined in the old aphorism "perspective must precede practice." We must begin with a right perspective. For marriage, the right perspective is set out in the Bible, where husbands and wives are called to focus on the glory of God. When they do, they will be ready to negotiate the practical challenges of marriage. But to begin with practical advice, with step-by-step remedies—where it seems many are eager to begin—is to anchor a union of enormous weight on a foundation of sand, to tackle the challenges of a rigorous ascent without the benefit of a sturdy rope. Sound practice, while certainly essential to healthy marriages, is only sound when it flows from right perspective.

It is helpful to examine exemplary marriages of the past. The nineteenth-century preacher Charles Spurgeon and his wife, Susannah, encountered many difficult obstacles in the course of their thirty-six years of marriage, including the trials of serious illness, debilitating depression, and scathing criticism in the national press. They met these disappointments with something more than anecdotal wisdom. In a poem of comfort written to his wife, Charles offered not tidbits of practical advice but solid perspective:

Though he who chose us all worlds before,
Must *reign* in our hearts alone,
We fondly believe that we shall adore,
Together before his throne.[3]

It is a perspective anchored in the sovereignty of God, in his loving reign over human lives, and it received a resounding echo in the thoughts of Susannah. After her husband's death, she reflected: "I can see two pilgrims treading the highway of life together, hand in hand, heart linked to heart. True they had mountains to climb, but their Guide was ever watchful. Mostly they went on their way singing."[4]

The challenges of life can be mountainous. With enough suffering to dismantle ten marriages, Charles and Susannah persevered and enjoyed many triumphs. How did they do it? What was their secret? They were sustained in their climb not in the first instance by pithy advice but by a perspective that "reigned in [their] hearts." It was the assurance that their "Guide" was able to convey them safely past the crags and crevices of life. And so they held on to him. They fixed their eyes on his glory.

When husbands and wives fasten their grips on the tether thrown down by the heavenly Guide, when they set their eyes on the awe-inspiring glory of God, they do more than pay lip service to a transcendent splendor with uncertain relevance to their lives. On the contrary, they cling to something that affects every dimension of their partnership, from their reactions in times of conflict to their celebrations in times of triumph. And they climb past the pitfalls of life with a song in their hearts. Of course they do! They climb with the assurance that one day their Guide will usher them all the way to the heavenly summit, where forever before the throne they will adore the Lord together.

It was mentioned at the outset of this book that the expectations of many marriages go unfulfilled. This is tragic and utterly unnecessary, especially if husbands and wives are prepared to adjust their perspectives and focus exclusively on the glory of the Lord.

But what does this mean? Where do we find divine glory?

We learned earlier that God's glory was clearly evident within the first marriage itself. In other words, the inaugural couple did not have to look far to find God's glory: it was radiating within their marriage. They needed only to cherish that glory, nurture it, and give it free reign in their lives. They needed to *live* for God's glory.

We must do the same thing. With the shared resolve of both partners, we must live for the glory of God.

But how?

3

CRUCIFORM LOVE

It appears that all that is ever spoken of in Scripture as an ultimate
end of God's works is included in that one phrase, the glory of God.

JONATHAN EDWARDS

By far the most prominent feature of our solar system is the sun. It
is a flaming colossus whose core temperature reaches an astonishing
15 million degrees centigrade. Fortunately, we receive only a minute
fraction of the energy produced in this nuclear furnace, otherwise we
would all face a very quick incineration! Yet great harm can still be
done to the eyes and skin of anyone not properly shielded from its
electromagnetic rays.

Given the sun's irradiating intensity, imagine how surprising it
would be if we were suddenly exhorted to live for the glory of this
bedazzling star. Such an exhortation would seem preposterous in the
extreme. How can mere mortals glorify an object of such incandescent splendor?

WHAT DOES IT MEAN TO GLORIFY GOD?
The process of giving glory to a luminous object is very straightforward. All that is required is *to reproduce a likeness of that object in such
a way as to illustrate its glory.*

At the moment these words are being written, Canada is com-
memorating the five-hundredth anniversary of the discovery of its
shores by the great Venetian explorer John Cabot. To illustrate the
glory of Cabot's achievement, the Canadian government has funded
the construction of a replica of his boat, the *Matthew*, staffed it with
a modern crew, and commissioned it to retrace the original voyage
from England to Newfoundland. On its arrival, the sailors will be
greeted by a thirteen-gun salute, the triumphant strains of bagpipes,

and a retinue of distinguished guests including Her Majesty the Queen. By presenting a mirror-like reproduction of the original achievement, Canadians will glorify a notable historical figure.

But how—on this understanding of what it means to glorify an earthly luminary—do we live to the glory of the extraterrestrial sun? How do we reproduce the likeness of something so incomprehensibly brilliant? How do we replicate the glory of a galactic wonder? Yet—and here is the stunning point of this solar excursus—we are asked to live to the glory of something more radiant than the sun. We are called to glorify One whose brightness reduces the star at the center of our solar system to a pale shadow. In our marriages, we are called to glorify the Creator of a billion suns!

We seldom contemplate the enormity of this challenge. Most Christians will admit that their chief calling is—according to the Westminster Confession—to glorify God and to enjoy him forever, but few can describe what this means. How *do* we glorify God? The question is essential for marriage. As we discovered above, the gem called matrimony sparkles its brightest when two partners are committed to glorifying their Maker.

THE IMAGE OF GOD

Human beings are well equipped to glorify God. We are created in God's image, a fact revealed in Genesis 1:26: "Let us make man in our image, after our likeness." We are made to reflect the likeness of God; and since his most salient feature is his glory, we must be able to reflect his glory. But that begs the question: What is the nature of the glory we are made to reflect? Much ink has been spilled on the subject, but answers remain elusive. A closer inspection of the biblical passage which launched our study of marriage can shed revealing light on the nature of God's glory.

In the first chapter of Genesis, God pours himself into the acts of creation. Over the course of six biblical days, he invests himself tirelessly in the birth of the universe and refuses to put down his tools until the last detail is finished. Finally, God "rested on the seventh day from all his work that he had done" (Gen. 2:2–3).

It is extraordinary that God should have devoted himself so fully to a work that could not possibly have added to his already perfect condition. His motive for creation must have been entirely selfless. He literally *gave himself up* to the work of creation.

In the next thousand or so pages of the Holy Scriptures, the self-giving nature of God becomes increasingly evident, especially as the biblical story ripens into the prophetic books and the New Testament. Inspired biblical authors are at pains to point out that "the steadfast love of the LORD never ceases; his mercies never come to an end" (Lam. 3:22).

The selflessness of God reaches a high point in the first century when, in an act of unparalleled selflessness, God lavished his Son on a rebellious world. The drama is captured with breathtaking simplicity by the apostle John: "For God so loved the world, that he *gave* his only Son" (John 3:16); and by the apostle Paul: God "did not spare his own Son but *gave* him up for us all" (Rom. 8:32). To the question What is the nature of God? we receive a clear biblical reply—he is extravagantly the self-giving One.

Ultimately, this attribute finds embodiment in the Son of God himself. In words reminiscent of Genesis 1, we are told that the divine Son, the man named Jesus, is the very image of God (Col. 1:15; 2 Cor. 4:4), the exact representation of God's being (Heb. 1:3), and the one in whom "the whole fullness of deity dwells" (Col. 2:9). If we seek greater insight into the nature of God, we must look carefully at the Son of God, the perfect revelation of the Father.

THE GLORY OF THE CROSS

Perhaps the most compelling description of the Son of God is found in the letter of Paul to the church at Philippi. With language again reminiscent of Genesis 1, the apostle composes an exalted tribute to Jesus Christ: because he existed in "the form of God" (a term nearly synonymous with "the image of God"), he did not use his lofty status as an opportunity for self-grasping but rather as a reason to empty himself, to humble himself, to take on "the form of a servant," and to submit to a slave's death, even the unthinkably repellent death of a cross (Phil. 2:6–8).

From the unspeakable riches of equality with God to the most impoverished death in antiquity, from heights unsearchable to depths unimaginable, from one polar extreme to another—this is the measure of the self-emptying of Jesus Christ. His death on a cross is history's most perfect expression of sacrificial love. And according to Paul, it is also the clearest revelation of what it means to be in the likeness of God. In Jesus, we see an image of the heavenly Father. On the cross, we behold a picture of infinite love.

We began with a simple question: What does it mean to glorify God? Many answers are suggested in the Bible. We glorify God when we praise him, when we delight in him, when we obey him. But we have seen there is a more dramatic answer: we glorify God when we reproduce a likeness of who he is. We now know what that likeness entails. More than any other person in history, Jesus presented a picture of God, and nowhere more clearly than in the event which crowned his earthly existence—his death on a cross. It was on that brutal and ignominious tree that we see the splendor of God's glory. Pointing to the cross, Jesus cried out: "The hour has come for the Son of Man to be glorified" (John 12:23).

Here is a monumental truth. The glory of God receives its fullest expression in the self-emptying love of the crucified Christ.

Cruciform love—that's God's glory!

How does this apply to us? In short, it spells out our calling as people made in God's image. We now possess a template for human existence. On the cross of Jesus Christ, we see not only an effulgence of divine glory but also how we as humans can replicate that glory— by exhibiting in our lives the same pattern of cruciform love that was embodied in the Lord's.

This insight into the glory of God sheds penetrating light on the very first command ever issued to human beings. Shortly after being endowed with the divine image, the man and the woman are enjoined to rule over creation (Gen. 1:26, 28). The same command is repeated in a slightly different form a few paragraphs later where

God instructs the pair to cultivate and "keep" the new garden home of Eden (Gen. 2:15). A close biblical link is thus forged between being endowed with God's image and ruling over creation, with the former clearly informing the latter. To be endowed with the image of God means to "rule" and "cultivate" and "keep" creation in a self-giving manner. Such selfless husbandry will transform an already exquisite creation into something even more beautiful.

A NEW KIND OF HELPER

The notion of "selfless husbandry" provides a ready link back to our main subject: the nature of biblical marriage. Applying the insights above to the relationship of husbands and wives, we can now see why the Lord concludes that "it is not good that the man should be alone" (Gen. 2:18)—a conclusion otherwise surprising given the earlier assessment that "everything that he had made . . . was very good" (1:31). The reason why the solitary existence of the man is not good is not because it forces the man to endure isolation and loneliness nor because he must face the challenges of life without human assistance—sentimental readings like these find little basis in the text—but because he has been endowed with the divine image and hence with the capacity to empty himself sacrificially into another. Such an endowment cannot be enjoyed unless there is at least one other person. For there to be an exchange of self-giving love, there must be duality within humanity. As a lone human, Adam cannot manifest the divine image.

For the man, there must be one who is "fit for him" (Gen. 2:18, 20), one who will match him as perfectly as the adjoining piece of a two-piece puzzle, one who will complement him by serving as the recipient of his self-emptying love. The unusual command to go out and give names to the animals was meant to convince man of this necessity. He discovered there was no one into whom he could pour himself. There was no "helper fit for him" (Gen. 2:20).

It should be obvious why perfect correspondence is necessary in a partner. There must be one who can receive what the man uniquely has to give, one capable of absorbing *his* love, one whose life he can nurture *as though it were his own*, one to whom he can give *his* name ("she shall be called Woman, because she was taken out of Man" [v. 23]), *his* loyalty ("a man shall leave his father and his mother" [v. 24]), *his* body ("a man shall . . . hold fast to his wife" [v. 24]), indeed *his* very life ("and they shall become one flesh" [v. 24]).

Woman, and woman alone, suffices! Only she can receive his *self*-giving love because only she possesses a self that corresponds to his. Imagine the alacrity of the man when, awakening from his "ribectomy," he beholds a creature who can receive his love. Here is the missing piece. Here is the perfect match. Here is a partner who corresponds to him. Here is one to whom he can give his name. Here is wo-*man*! He celebrates the discovery with an ecstatic soliloquy: "This at last is bone of *my* bones and flesh of *my* flesh" (Gen. 2:23)!

Yet it is easy to miss the point of his elation. A young schoolgirl was once asked why God created Eve, and she responded precociously: "After making Adam, God felt he could do better. That's why he created Eve!" We can sympathize with her reply. The identity of the fairer sex is hardly open to dispute. Yet it is not the allurements typically associated with feminine beauty that prompt the initial celebration. It is not her physical form, nor her sage intuition, nor her uncanny wit. It is rather her capacity to assist the man in fulfilling his creaturely vocation. Because of her, the man can now manifest the divine likeness. He can express self-giving love. He can enter into the wonder of being human. He can radiate the image of God. He can glorify God.

This explains why God created woman as "a helper" (Gen. 2:18). She provides indispensable assistance to her male counterpart. Without her, the image of God would lie dormant. The arrival of Eve provides Adam with the most important help of all. She assists him, not primarily by sharing the load of domestic duties or by providing emotional support when his mood flags, but more importantly by providing a context in which he can venture a full expression of his humanity. She becomes the recipient of his self-giving love.

Similarly, the man "helps" the woman. She also bears the image of God (Gen. 1:27) and becomes all God intends her to be only when there is another into whom she can pour her own self-giving love. (This important truth is as relevant to the single person as it is to married couples, as we shall see in chapter 11.)

This brings us to a remarkable discovery. Implicit in the narrative account of creation is a principle vital to the success of every marriage. Put succinctly, we marry for the good of our partner. This is a radical notion and quite different from the incentives normally governing marriage. Typically, we marry for what a person will give to us, hence what we will become by virtue of sharing life with that person. We often interpret the word "helper" in Genesis 2 as one who gives us assistance in any of a number of different ways, from increasing our incomes to producing our progeny.

But if we are right in our understanding of the word, its meaning is nearly the opposite. A helper is one who receives *our* assistance, and so helps us to reflect the image of God. In short, husbands and wives marry in order *to give themselves to their helper.* (The application of this truth to both husbands and wives will become evident when, in chapters 5 and 6, we consider Paul's teaching in Ephesians 5.)

HEAVEN ON EARTH

When this principle is comprehended and prayerfully applied, the result is a marriage which begins to look like a bit of heaven on earth. The glory of God in the shape of cruciform love inundates such a union. On the other hand, when this principle is neglected, it becomes the source of every marital problem. Yes—*every* problem! Every instance of marital discord and every disruption of marital tranquility can be traced directly to the failure to apply this fundamental principle. When one spouse endeavors, not to give to the other, but to take from the other—by insisting that the other do more, care more, listen more, change more, communicate more, give more—marital friction is the inevitable result. But when partners concentrate on giving themselves to the other for the good of the other, their marriage begins to shine with the glory of heaven.

But it is not just marriage that shines. Society as a whole reaps a huge dividend. When self-giving love effervesces within marriages, the condition of the entire human race improves. The earthly garden is well watered. Children who emerge from self-giving marriages will tend, on the whole, to radiate the image of God. Raised in an atmosphere where mothers and fathers relate to each other through expressions of sacrificial love, children will also reflect that love, growing up to "rule" and "cultivate" and "keep" their own corners of the earth with a parallel commitment to selfless sacrifice. And when they do, creation flourishes.

We can now appreciate the rationale underlying the assertion that marriage represents a high point of creation. What could bring greater glory to God than the dissemination of his self-giving image throughout the whole earth? When God's love spreads to the four corners of the earth, it creates a cohesion within creation that brings glory to his name.

An important vehicle of that cohesion is marriage. To the first couple came the divine imperative: "Be fruitful and multiply and fill the earth and subdue it" (Gen. 1:28). In other words, fill the planet with marriages which bear the imprint of the image of God and with children who are marked by exposure to that image. Let the earth be "subdued" through the multiplication of God-glorifying progeny! For modern environmentalists, it sounds like a prescription for overpopulation. For those with the insight of Scripture, it represents the sweetest ecological note ever sounded. The far-flung migration of marriages manifesting the self-giving love of the Creator will produce great fruitfulness. God-glorifying marriages create a healthy world.

But our world is not healthy. It is infected at every turn by division and strife. What does the blight of interpersonal discord suggest except that the fundamental building block of society, marriage, is crumbling? When nearly 90 percent of marital unions are regarded by both partners as chronically dissatisfying, when there are nearly one and a quarter million divorces annually in the United States (a rate of marital breakdown 700 percent greater than that of a century ago), when over half of all US children eighteen years old and younger live in homes where at least one natural parent is missing, when "what has been shown over and over again to contribute most to the emotional development of the child—a close, warm, sustained and continuous relationship with both parents"—is often lacking,[1] when marital unions fail to exhibit even a modicum of the self-giving likeness of the Creator, the consequences socially will be devastating. When marriages crumble, societies crumble.

Ministering to the World

Several important lessons emerge from these reflections. First of all, we must come to regard matrimony as something bigger than merely a relationship between two individuals. It is more than husbands and wives "sharing life together." Rather, it is a relationship shared with the world, a relationship designed by God to administer universally the balm of his self-giving love. Whenever we love our spouse, we nurture the world.

Because marriage is so strategic socially, husbands and wives ought to ask themselves in conversations together at the dinner table, in bed before turning out the lights, and while driving in the car: Are we, as marriage partners, glorifying God? Do we, as husband and wife, seek to express his self-giving image to each other? Are we, together, providing an exhibition of cruciform love within our world? Do we, by the way we relate to each other, offer a solution to the social ills of our day? Are we, in our regular prayers together, asking God to sustain us in this lofty vocation? We should ask questions like these as though life on our planet depended on them. Because it does!

Identifying Selfishness

Secondly, whenever discord arises between husbands and wives, the remedy is straightforward. It begins with the recognition that every rift can be traced to a single cause: the failure to express self-giving love. In one or both partners selflessness has been gobbled up by selfishness.

None of us, no matter how spiritually mature we may be, is immune to selfishness. On this side of heaven, self-centeredness is a burr in the saddle of even the most devout couples. But the implicit challenge of the biblical passages above is to be vigilant in identifying that selfishness, and not primarily in the heart of our partner but in our *own* heart. The defects of a spouse must never be our first order of business. When divisions erupt, we must ask whether we can detect any selfishness in our own hearts and then ask God to renew within us the humble love that characterizes his image. Such a prayer will not go unanswered.

But how should a partner respond when he or she succeeds at loving the other but is met in return by indifference, unkindness, or even cruelty? Do such rebuffs give license to withdraw our affections, to indulge in self-pity, or worse, to respond in kind? No! Rather, they provide opportunities to become even more selfless in our love. Like Christ, whose sacrificial love shone brightest when it was poured into those who gave him greatest offense, our love is most radiant when it is expressed in trying circumstances. The selfishness of one partner opens a door for the other to become even more like our self-emptying God and hence even more expressive of his glory.

When disagreements arise in marriage, it is tempting to become defensive. Seldom are we willing to assess blame to ourselves, especially when a dispute is still burning hot or when words and actions have inflicted deep wounds or when our position is being assailed and we are reticent to back down. At times such as these, we are quick to imagine that the other party is guilty. Why? Is it because we nurture in our minds memories of our partner's past failures and suspect a repetition of those failures? Is it because we have grown weary of the way our partner deals with (or perhaps avoids) disappointments, and we lack the will (or the patience) to talk through matters until a positive resolution is achieved?

Impatience is a sure sign that we have forfeited the first principle of marriage. So is a critical spirit. So is a lack of tenderness. So are harsh words. So is anger. Each of these indicates we are no longer seeking to glorify God by spending ourselves on behalf of our partner.

It is important to ask the following questions: Are we giving ourselves up to, or seeking to receive from, our partner? Are we willing to relinquish our rights, our opinions, our pride, our correctness, our fears, and our personal comforts to minister to our partner? Are we willing to look past a curt or a cruel response and to labor instead to build up our spouse? When we can answer questions like these affirmatively, we know the glory of God is taking hold of our marriages.

Imaging Humility

Thirdly, we must remain constantly aware of what by now ought to be very clear, that our marriages flourish best when both spouses are marked by a large influx of humility.

The glory of God is always manifested in humility. Earlier we noticed that Adam was commanded to give names to the living creatures. It proved to be a defining moment for him. Acknowledging that no animal was found to correspond to him, Adam was compelled to admit his own incompleteness. He was only one piece of a two-piece puzzle, and the adjoining piece was nowhere in sight. He was surrounded, unhappily, by snails, giraffes, snakes, and geese. The awareness of his aloneness, indeed of his incompleteness, must have been profoundly humbling.

Humility is bedrock for successful marriages. We must view ourselves as incomplete apart from the one to whom we give ourselves in love. How humbling! And how easily we can jettison this insight for a misplaced confidence in our own ability to manage life apart from our spouse.

Too often as husbands and wives we seek our completeness in other things—our job, our children, our hobbies. But in marriage we are called to find our completeness in the sacrificial nurture of our partner. We must be wise enough to recognize this calling and humble enough to embrace it. We must confess our need, not in the first instance to receive from, but to give to our partner.

THE PRIORITY OF "BEING" OVER "DOING"

Doubtless the overarching insight arising from Genesis 1 and 2 is this: marriage is not ultimately something we do but something we are. It is not primarily the performance of a list of duties or roles. It cannot be reduced to a series of steps or procedures. That is why this book did not begin with the how-tos of marriage.

Instead, marriage is something we are to the glory of One more resplendent than the sun. We are created in his image. We are made in his likeness. In marriage, we are an illustration of what the Lord is himself, a radiant beacon of self-giving love. We glorify God by being what we are in Christ, people who present a replica of the sacrificial service adorning the crucified Lord.

When a husband and a wife reproduce the glory of God in their relationship, they elicit songs of praise from the angels. They also take steps on earth, very practical steps, up the slopes of marital completeness. Right perspective leads to sound practice. When two partners climb together for the glory of the Lord, their ascent—indeed their every step—advances toward the summit.

4

TRANSFORMATION

What a lot of trouble there is in marriage! Think of all the squabbles Adam and Eve must have had in the course of their nine hundred years. Eve would say, "You ate the fruit," and Adam would retort, "You gave it to me."

MARTIN LUTHER

Every child is enchanted by a rainbow. Hanging like a glistening arch across a darkened sky, transposing a familiar landscape into a glowing wonderland, intoxicating the senses with bold stripes of iridescent color—it is the epitome of childhood dreams. Little girls and boys always rush headlong toward the beckoning beam no matter how pelting the rain in the hope of bathing in its brilliant hues and unearthing the pot of gold. And who can blame them? Pity the adult who must douse the dream in a bucket of cold reality: "You will never find it. Rainbows are always beyond our reach."

The biblical vision of marriage is no less enchanting. Two people transfixed by the glory of God and replicating that glory by passing back and forth expressions of cruciform love, imaging the radiance of the Lord to all who intersect their path—marriage can be a glowing wonderland, a heaping pot of gold, a beacon of light amid a bleak landscape.

But we must ask ourselves: How often does reality conform to the ideal? Where are the marriages that consistently project an image of the Lord's glory? They are "rare," observed Martin Luther, canvassing the marriages of his countrymen five centuries ago. They may be even rarer today. We live in what many identify as a postmarital culture, where the biblical view of marriage, with its bold stripes of iridescent color, seems like a childish dream beyond our reach.

WHAT UNDERMINES MARRIAGE

The erosion of the marital ideal actually began with the very first couple. Not long after Adam and Eve received "the keys" to their garden paradise, they made an unhappy discovery. Their marital union, which had been defined by expressions of mutual self-giving love, was vulnerable to a very different impulse: the self-centered cravings of two individuals. Seeing "that the tree was good for food, and . . . a delight to the eyes, and that the tree was to be desired to make one wise, she *took* of its fruit and ate, and she also gave some to her husband who was with her, and he ate" (Gen. 3:6).

The man and the woman thus became *self*-grasping, plucking fruit from the one tree God had forbidden. They were driven to this sin by the impulse of *self*-interest. They saw that the tree was able to make them wise. As a consequence, they became *self*-conscious. "They sewed fig leaves together and made themselves loincloths" (Gen. 3:7). Finally, they became *self*-defensive. "The man said [to the Lord God], 'The woman whom you gave to be with me, she gave me fruit of the tree, and I ate'" (Gen. 3:12).

In short, they became conscious of their individual *selves*. What had been a seamless union bound together by *self*-forgetful love now dissolved into a fractured duality. The innocence of oneness was displaced by two people ashamed of their naked *selves*. Life as they knew it, full of the Creator's glory, disintegrated into a brooding darkness. Each partner withheld him-*self* or her-*self* from the other, concealing behind leaves the *selves* once given to the other so freely.

What went wrong? In a very real sense, we have been trying to answer the question ever since. What sabotages the unity between husbands and wives? Modern analysts have pointed to three factors.

Gender Discord

The first is the social observation that the gap between the genders is simply too large and makes irreconcilable differences inevitable. As ancient mythology reminds us, men are from Mars (the god of war) and women from Venus (the goddess of love). The sexes could scarcely be more different, as dissimilar as love and war. Cynics have exploited this chasm by composing clever witticisms: "How men hate waiting while their wives shop for clothes and trinkets; how women hate waiting while their husbands shop for fame and glory."[1] The divide between male and female inevitably sows seeds of discord.

Easy Dissolution

There is an additional factor causing marital disharmony, and it arises from the halls of jurisprudence. Until recently, the legal system protected the sanctity of marriage and made dissolution a long and arduous process. Times have changed. Now laws permit easy termination of marriage and protect as an almost sacred privilege the right to separate. Divorce attorneys, once unknown, are ubiquitous; and the possibility of procuring the services of a lawyer to *preserve* a marriage has become a laughable anomaly. What was once the most binding of social covenants—irrevocable "till death do us part"—is now a very fragile contract, dissoluble on almost any grounds at all. Easy divorce has become a disincentive to resolving marital conflicts.

Annoying Differences

The third factor undermining modern marriage arises from the realm of psychology. An increasingly sophisticated battalion of therapists has identified a series of influences, inherited and environmental, which renders the union of two personalities challenging at best and impossible at worst. The sheer number of psychological flaws inherent within partners lead many therapists to conclude that, in especially stressed relationships, marital oneness is a futile hope and divorce a reasonable option. When this sort of fatalistic advice is allowed to influence the courses of marriages, when suspicion is planted in one partner that the annoying traits of the other are unlikely to be amended, a strong bias in favor of separation is created. "I came to realize I just could not change him (or her)," is the refrain of many dying marriages.

Here, then, are three factors contributing to the failure of modern marriages: the social (genders are too different), the legal (laws are too lenient), and the psychological (personalities are too incompatible). Together they present a formidable axis against matrimony.

Yet none of them—nor all of them together—presents the greatest threat to husbands and wives. Ultimately, marriages founder not because two people are different but because they share a common defect; not because of the leniency of civil laws but because of the stridency of uncivil hearts; and not because of grating personalities but because of corruption in the innermost being. For the deeper cause of marital problems, we must look again at the biblical account of the first marriage.

THE DEFECT OF THE FIRST MARRIAGE

It is no secret what unraveled the marriage of Adam and Eve: it was disobedience. God had offered the newlyweds the enjoyment of any tree of the garden—any, that is, except the tree of the knowledge of good and evil. Of its charms they were to remain blissfully ignorant (Gen. 2:16–17). Nevertheless, they ate of the forbidden fruit, and the reason they did was because they saw the fruit as a springboard to personal enhancement (Gen. 3:6).

It was the allure of personal nourishment (she saw that the tree was good for food), personal pleasure (that it was a delight to the eyes), and personal wisdom (that it could make one wise) that prompted the couple to disobey God. In other words, they succumbed to the desire to take charge of their own destinies, promote their own well-being, and rebel against the Master of their existence. It is a desire the Bible calls sin, a yearning to usurp the position of God by becoming the master of one's own destiny. It is a betrayal of our created purpose.

We were fashioned by God to glorify God. We were created to exhibit his self-emptying love. But at a seminal point in history, our forebearers, Adam and Eve, sought to glorify themselves. Their problem was not merely that they did something wrong. It was deeper than that. They were twisted at the cores of their beings. The orientation of their hearts was tragically inward and self-grasping, rather than upward and self-giving. It was the opposite of right.

So it has been for all of us. The first couple's error is every person's downfall. As the apostle Paul reminds us: "Sin came into the world through one man," and now "all have sinned and fall short of the glory of God" (Rom. 5:12; 3:23). Inheriting Adam's nature, we participate in his folly. At our roots, we are self-promoting. In our deeds, we are self-serving. And the consequences are devastating.

Every earthly ill may be traced to this Adamic defect. Every instance of interpersonal abuse, every report of racial strife, every episode of international discord, indeed every thought or deed falling short of the self-giving love of God is a product of our ancestral link to Adam. It ought to be obvious. Early in the last century, the British essayist G. K. Chesterton commented: "The one philosophy empirically validated by thirty-five hundred years of recorded human history is the doctrine of original sin."[2]

The ugly-sounding carbuncle called "sin" has attached itself to our *innermost beings*—prompting us to seek our own glory instead of God's—and has infected our *outward deeds*—inciting us to serve ourselves instead of others.

THE SHATTERING CONSEQUENCES OF SIN

The consequences of sin for marriage, in which two people live in such close proximity, are venomous. Husbands and wives, both seeking their own enhancement—how can this not hinder, if not shatter, a union?

Men Exploiting Women

The prophetic utterance addressed to Eve at the moment of her sin has become the experience of every marriage: "Your desire shall be for your husband, and he shall rule over you" (Gen. 3:16). Indeed, husbands *have* ruled over their wives. They have ridden roughshod over the needs and feelings of their partners. Not even the largest and most prolonged advocacy movement in modern history, the crusade of women in the West to obtain treatment equal to that of men, has been able to put an end to male domination. Even today women are exploited in boardrooms and bedrooms—and tragically in marriages.

History traces a pathetic trail of male chauvinism. Plato believed that a bad man's fate was to be reincarnated as a woman.[3] Aristotle taught that "females are imperfect males, accidentally produced by the father's inadequacy or by the malign influence of a moist south wind."[4] Josephus believed that "the woman is inferior to the man in every way."[5] In the Jewish Talmud, men are taught to give thanks that God did not make them "a Gentile, a slave, or a woman."[6] In Gandhi's autobiography, "a Hindu husband regards himself as lord and master of his wife, who must ever dance attendance upon him."[7] In the Koran, "men have authority over women because Allah has made the one superior to the other."[8] There is an unbroken tradition of male domination in both the East and the West.[9] The sad prophecy of Genesis 3:16—"he shall rule over you"—has been confirmed by history.

Women Mastering Men

What of the first half of the prophecy and the cryptic phrase "your desire shall be for your husband"? Traditionally, biblical scholars have interpreted the word *desire* to refer to the female sexual drive, no doubt because childbirth is mentioned in the sentence immediately preceding (Gen. 3:16). This gives the rendering: despite the travails of labor and delivery, a wife will nevertheless desire sexual intimacy with her husband.

However accurate a description of the female sex drive, it represents a dubious interpretation of the text. The Hebrew word for *desire* occurs only one other place in Genesis, in the account of Cain and Abel. There the Lord reproves Cain for his murderous intentions: Sin's "*desire* is for you, but you must rule over it" (4:7). Here the word *desire* has nothing to do with the sexual drive; it is rather a passion, engendered by sin, to obtain mastery over a brother. It is doubtless this same sin which explains the woman's desire in Genesis 3. It is a desire to gain mastery over the husband.

On this interpretation, it is clear that the first half of the prophecy in Genesis 3:16 has also received a disturbing fulfillment. Women who have grown weary of male domination have, often with good reason, sought to master men. This is especially apparent in modern times. The age-old pattern of women offering unquestioned subservience to their husbands in exchange for the material support of both themselves and their children has, in the last half century, undergone seismic revision.

Women are now increasingly their own masters. They chart their own courses. With the advent of reliable birth control in the form of contraception and abortion, women can dictate the frequency and the timing of childbearing. With increasing participation in the higher echelons of the workforce, women can also provide for their own and their children's own maintenance. By creating their own identity and asserting emotional independence, the female desire to master men has become a reality of modern life.

But at what cost? The answer is evident in many contemporary marriages—at a cost almost unbearable! The twin impulses of husbands seeking to rule over their wives and of wives seeking to master their husbands have brought marital expeditions to such a low level—barely above base camp and the initial bliss of the wedding—that many couples have little conception of the prize they are forfeiting.

On a broader social level, the cost is equally tragic. The relationship which was meant to be the basis of healthy societies, providing a steady stream of the self-giving love of the Creator and drawing the earth into a harmonious whole, has lost its redemptive power. The absence of the glory of God in marriage is a catastrophic loss indeed. And it is all because of the insidious inner passion that seeks its own interests above the interests of another. In the case of the husband, it is exploitation of the "top position," and in the case of the wife, it is a quest for the "top position."

It is important to be very clear about the internal flaw shared by both genders. What undermines marriages is not primarily the presence of lamentable social, legal, or psychological influences. It is rather the absence of self-giving love. That is what impoverishes marital partnerships. Until we find a solution to what the Scriptures call "sin," the marital rainbow beckoning with its enchanting hues will remain forever beyond our grasp.

THE GOD WHO SAVES OUR MARRIAGES

Here our examination of marriage might grind to a screeching halt were it not for the reality that God's love for sinners is stronger than his condemnation of sin. To be sure, the heavenly Father abominates sin. It represents a personal affront, diminishing his glory and effacing the radiance of men and women created in his image. What good father would not be enraged by the sinful disintegration of his children? And who would blame such a father if, in his wrath, he allowed his offspring to suffer the consequences of their rebellion?

Yet astonishingly, our father, the heavenly Father, keeps his eyes peeled to the horizon awaiting our return, awaiting our repentance. And when we do turn around, even while a long way off, he sees us and, filled with compassion, runs to us, throws his arms around us, kisses us, and says: Let's have a feast and celebrate. For this child of mine was dead but is alive again, was lost but is now found (Luke 15:20, 23–24).

It is a reunion that touches us deeply. Yet more is happening here than first meets the eye. The ravaged image of humanity is clearly intolerable to the eyes of the Maker, and so in an expression of love quantum leaps beyond any other instance in history, he draws us up into his very constitution, embracing us warts and all, pulling us so far into himself that he seems actually to be taking on our human flesh. Indeed he is! In a mystery that boggles the minds of angels, a mystery we call the incarnation, the Creator climbs into the flesh of his creatures and becomes like those who were meant to be like him, those who in their sin have become the exact opposite of him (John 1:14).

Why does he do this?

In order to renew us according to his image!

Such a radical makeover can only be accomplished one way: by the overthrow of sin. It is a conquest more costly than that of any other undertaking. What begins with incarnation in a feeding trough proceeds to annihilation on a criminal's cross. Yes, the Immortal dies! In the Son of God, the eternal Father tastes death. And it is a death we ought to have died. Instead—and here history reaches a breath-taking crescendo—the Son dies in our place, paying the penalty of our sins, debiting them from our account and crediting them to his, and (as a result) imputes to us his own perfect righteousness.

The infinitely costly work of the cross thus purchases for us the absolutely free gift of God's righteousness. We are—irrevocably and forever—put right by Jesus Christ. Or in terms relevant to the subject of husbands and wives, the self-centeredness which riddles every marriage is precisely the defect which Christ bears to the killing tree, removing it from us and cloaking us with his righteousness and—perhaps most marvelously of all—reconnecting us to our heavenly Father.

This last provision, reconnecting us to the heavenly Father, is the key to the renewal of our marriages. Reconnected to God, we can be refilled by his matchless love. In other words, the death of our sins in the death of Jesus Christ has an even greater object in view than the removal of those sins: namely, the birth within us of a new way to be human.

The shackles of the cross proved no match for the power of Christ. He exploded from the tomb, arose from the dead, and bore in his arms a life no longer manacled to sin and death but liberated to a new existence according to divine image. Because of the resurrection of Jesus Christ, we can now reflect the glory of the Lord's cruciform love. Or as Paul announces triumphantly, we can "put on the new self, which is being renewed in knowledge after the image of its creator" (Col. 3:10), a new existence in which we no longer live for ourselves but for him who died and rose for us (2 Cor. 5:15).

The implications of the death and resurrection of Jesus Christ are staggering. The one who is "in Christ" is a miracle of new creation; the old self-serving ways have passed away and new self-emptying passions have taken their place (2 Cor. 5:17). The stranglehold of sin has been broken, its penalty paid, its power purged. We are resurrected to the likeness of the Creator himself, reflecting the love of the crucified Christ and thus radiating his glory.

Once dead to God's purposes, we are now alive to them. Once lost, we are now found. Once imprisoned by sin, we are now freely human. "Let's have a feast and celebrate!"

In Christ, then, hope for marriage is resuscitated. Matchless peaks of the marital relationship once again come into view. The iridescent rainbow with its pot of gold is no longer merely a fantasy. It can be found. God *can* be glorified in our marriages. Marital oneness *can* become a vehicle of blessing to the world. All this is now possible . . . *if* God calls us by name, runs to us, and embraces us as his children; *if* God adopts us anew in Jesus Christ; *if* we respond to his call by turning around, confessing our self-centeredness, repenting of sin, and returning home to the Father; *if* we entrust our lives to the work of the cross and resurrection of Christ; *if* we commit our destinies to the Guide who can sustain us in a triumphant marital ascent; *if* we cling to him for the success of our marriages.

Is this your response to the gospel of Jesus Christ? Have you, as husband and wife, trusted Christ as your Savior from sin and as the Lord of your lives? No two people who venture their all on Christ will ever be disappointed.

THE TRANSFORMING WORK OF CHRIST

Several lessons emerge from the biblical vision of a re-created humanity. First of all, matrimony is an intensely spiritual relationship. Secular counsel will find it difficult to lift marital unions above the din of self-interest. The best human advice may bring momentary relief, but it can never produce a sustained marital ascent. We need more. Much more! We need a miracle of transformation at the core of our beings, a miracle only Christ can perform.

The Power of the Spirit

This point can hardly be stressed enough. Marital partnerships need renewing by a supernatural work of God's Spirit. Recently a friend whose marriage was at the point of collapse returned from the therapist with an optimistic report: "The counselor really made me feel better about myself." Although the words were encouraging on one level, they were the equivalent of spreading icing on a moldy cake. While tasty, it camouflages a deeper problem. While putting my friend in touch with her feelings, it does not put her in touch with her God. While making her feel good about herself, it does not in fact make her good.

It is only when we confess the spiritual nature of our marital problems—the internal defect at the core of our beings—that we will yearn for the supernatural assistance offered by Christ. We need a makeover of our inmost hearts, a coronary transformation by the healing touch of the Spirit of Christ.

Since supernatural help is available in abundance, the following affirmation is true: no marriage, regardless of how impaired, is ever beyond repair. Emotionally frayed partners may scoff at this affirmation. Staggering along in ruts painfully deep and years wide, pessimism can become entrenched. But the God who can turn something as ugly as a crucifixion into something as beautiful as a resurrection can surely provide for the revival of our marriages.

When the power of the resurrection is applied to the hearts of husbands and wives, even the worst interpersonal fractures can be mended. Greater is the Spirit in us than anything that might unhinge our marriages. Our prayers for marriage—are we praying?—can be bathed in the assurance that the God who hears our prayers is strong enough to overcome any difficulty.

The Battle against Sin

It would be wrong, however, to imagine that marriages can achieve complete perfection. While the victory of the cross is certainly complete and self-centeredness and sin have been dealt a mortal blow, the work of the cross has not yet been fully implemented, nor will it be fully implemented until the day the Lord returns. There are still pockets of resistance, even in the hearts of those who are in Christ. The most faithful believer will continue to struggle with self-centered desires, and so will the most Christ-centered marriage.

Self-giving love is not an instant attainment; rather, it is a process not unlike metamorphosis. According to Paul, when we look at the glory of the Lord, we are transformed [the word in Greek is *metamorpheo*] into the very same image, from one stage of glory to the next (2 Cor. 3:18). The metamorphosis of the Christian is decidedly upward, with self-centeredness giving way progressively to the self-emptying love of the Lord.

And when selfishness does rear its ugly head, it can be turned into an opportunity for spiritual growth, especially when it sends couples to their knees asking God to continue the process of metamorphosis. When we implore him for what he alone can supply—greater increments of self-giving love—and when we ask him buoyed by the assurance that this is precisely what he wants to supply, he will supply.

Partners in marriage ought not to be surprised, then, when lingering egocentrism undermines their union—grieved, yes, but not surprised. Here it is vital to maintain a careful balance. Sometimes husbands and wives will grieve too much over their self-centeredness and be pummeled by incapacitating guilt. They need to remember that their self-seeking passions will only fully be eradicated at the return of Christ, when those who are in Christ will at last be fully conformed to the image of their Savior (Phil. 3:20–21). It is comforting to sensitive consciences to know that earthly perfection is beyond reach.

Alternatively, husbands and wives may grieve too little over self-centered ways and dismiss their sin—almost cavalierly—as the unavoidable symptom of their still-corrupted flesh. They do not express enough surprise at behavior contrary to their position in Christ and need to be jolted out of their malaise.

Incapacitating guilt and cavalier indifference are polar mechanisms of coping with the problem of sin—the first making too much of the problem, the second too little. But human methods of coping are always inadequate. Only God, through the death and resurrection of Jesus Christ, can overturn our sin. We must humbly turn to him. Those inclined to be indifferent should weep with alarm—"*Oh my*, I am a helpless sinner!"—and those riddled by guilt should smile in embarrassment—"*Of course*, I am a helpless sinner!" In this fashion, we abandon human devices and lean entirely on the Savior.

THE BALM OF CONFESSION

It is so important whenever disharmony arises between husbands and wives quickly to recognize the true nature of the problem: it is the sin of self-centeredness. Sadly, we often recoil from such an acknowledgment. We are more inclined to identify superficial irritants like incompatible personalities, trying circumstances, or differing opinions. But it is rarely the irritants themselves, rather the way sin exploits those irritants, that causes conflict in marriage.

Gratefully—as we have seen—there is a solution. No matter how deep the difficulties, two people can be restored to the process of becoming more like Christ by confessing their self-centeredness and soliciting the work of the master Sculptor whose hand chisels away the abrasive edges of the internal defect. Marital difficulties, far from debilitating, can foster spiritual growth. They can drive us to the Savior.

So much depends on a willingness to admit the deeper problem. It is an admission which itself requires a miracle of the Holy Spirit, especially when two people are already feuding and neither is willing to concede an inch. It takes courageous humility to withdraw the finger pointed accusingly at the partner and redirect it onto oneself, a humility the Spirit of Christ can engender in our hearts.

It is incumbent on married couples to stay close to the Holy Spirit. We must present ourselves regularly to his humbling breezes. We must run up the sails every day to catch anew the full force of his powerful winds. We must avoid the doldrums, steering clear of anything that might diminish spiritual refreshment, becoming so convinced of our need for heavenly assistance that we discipline ourselves to look intently at the glory of the Lord and feast on the revelation of Jesus Christ in the Holy Scriptures. It is a discipline that the Holy Spirit will use to transform us into the image of the Lord, from one degree of glory to the next (2 Cor. 3:18).

May it be the blessing of every couple reading these words to immerse themselves in the Holy Scriptures, drawing inspiration from its matchless portrait of Jesus Christ. The intake of biblical truth will be used by the Spirit for transformation, bringing the marital dream of many hues to reality, producing a union in which there is, so to speak, neither male nor female, just a seamless fusion of two people in Christ.

PART TWO

LOVE WITHIN MARRIAGE

5

A WIFE'S SPIRIT

Charm is deceitful, and beauty is vain, but a woman who fears the
Lord is to be praised. Give her of the fruit of her hands, and let
her works praise her in the [city] gates.

KING SOLOMON

There is a surprising scarcity of biblical instruction devoted specifically to marriage. In the many letters of the apostle Paul, for
instance, we find only two pieces of advice to married couples—
one word directed to wives and one to husbands. Does the pau-
city of teaching on the important subject of marriage represent
the oversight of a disinterested bachelor, or has Paul honed his
advice to two priceless gems? We shall discover that it is the latter. Notwithstanding the endless volumes of marital instruction
authored since biblical times, it is still these two golden nuggets
which, if embraced and followed by both partners, will produce a
marriage that reflects the glory of heaven.

WHY SUBMISSION?

We will begin where Paul himself begins, with the single piece of
advice to married women. "Wives, submit to your husbands," (Eph.
5:22; Col. 3:18). The key term here is of course the imperative "submit." It comes from the Greek word *hupotasso*, a compound term
made up of two parts, a preposition *hupo*, which means "under," and
a verbal form *tasso*, which may be translated "to line up." Putting the
two together produces the literal rendering: "to line up under." The
expression was originally used in military contexts of conscripts who
would line up under their commanding officer. The most accurate
English translation would probably be the term "to sub-ordinate."

According to Paul, the most helpful piece of wisdom he can offer to wives is to subordinate themselves to their husbands.

To contemporary ears the injunction sounds highly inflammatory, if not medieval. Over the last hundred years, women have waged a tireless battle to throw off the unjust shackles of male domination. Their conquests have been hard won, and throughout the campaign the rallying cry has been: "No more subordination!" To them the apostle's word represents a cruel anachronism. It makes a mockery of the sacrifices of brave suffragettes and marks a return to chauvinistic abuses only recently repelled.

Yet we must not be too hasty in our disparagement of Paul. Nor should we listen to an ancient text like Ephesians 5 through the emotional megaphone of modern debates on the equality of genders. Grappling with words written two millennia ago, we must seek to hear them through the ears of the original audience. If we do so, a remarkable discovery awaits us.

The first century was a time when, not unlike our own, women were asserting their rights and climbing to positions of social prominence. The injunction to subordinate themselves to their husbands would have sounded as reactionary to their ears as it does to ours. Surely the apostle was aware of the provocative nature of his counsel. This is the same man who on other occasions campaigned on behalf of women's rights, even coining the revolutionary slogan: "There is no male and female, for you are all one in Christ Jesus" (Gal. 3:28). How do we reconcile Paul's advocacy on behalf of women to his jarring command to wives?

There is a simple solution. It is possible that the injunction "wives submit to your husbands" was not intended to be demeaning at all. It may even have been intended to exalt the position of wives.

Many interpreters of Paul have failed to reckon with this possibility. Too often they explain the injunction of subordination in terms of the sociological reality that human relationships typically follow prescribed orders of hierarchy. By encouraging wives to subordinate themselves to their husbands, Paul is identifying a clear stratification within marriage. In times of disagreement or in moments of important decision, the husband must take the lead, and the wife must defer to his leadership.

But there is an obvious weakness to this interpretation. Its application is severely limited in scope. Seldom do healthy partnerships descend into intractable disagreements, and seldom are important decisions made without mutual consent. It would be surprising—to say nothing of dispiriting—if the one piece of marital advice offered to wives is applicable only in rare instances when partnerships arrive at loggerheads.

THE EXALTATION OF SUBMISSION

The contexts of Ephesians 5 and Colossians 3 suggest a more likely interpretation. In both cases, the apostle Paul qualifies the injunction with a comparative clause: "Wives, submit to your own husbands, *as to the Lord*" (Eph. 5:22); "Wives, submit to your husbands, *as is fitting in the Lord*" (Col. 3:18). The emphasis of each clause falls on the term *Lord*. The interpretive key to the controversial injunction is thus not the insights of modern sociology but rather something far more profound and far more personal—the relationship of wives to the Lord.

It is a relationship marked by love, perfect and unconditional love—in the first instance, the love which the Lord pours into the hearts of wives (Rom. 5:5). And because wives are recipients of this massive love, they respond—naturally and gratefully—by subordinating themselves to the Lord.

In their subordination, wives take a cue from the Lord's own subordination to his Father. According to Paul, Christ became obedient (a near synonym of *subordinate*) to the point of death (Phil. 2:6–8). But his submission did not relegate him to a position of inferiority; on the contrary, it won him the most coveted prize in the universe. "God has highly exalted him and bestowed on him the name that is above every name" (Phil. 2:9).

Exaltation by subordination! It is a lesson with special relevance to wives. When wives subordinate themselves to their husbands in the same way as the Lord subordinated himself to his Father, they, too, can win a coveted prize. Far from chafing under the stigma of submission, they can soar to places of honor.

PROACTIVE SUBORDINATION

What does a wife's subordination look like in practice? In short, it bears a striking resemblance to her subordination to the Lord. She submits to her husband "as to the Lord" (Eph. 5:22)—in other words, in the same way as she submits to the Lord. Since she is more than the Lord's slave, her submission entails more than mere acquiescence in times of disagreement or decision. Since she is his beloved child, she responds to him as to a cherished parent, seeking in every way and at all times to honor him, to please him, to respect him, to exalt him, and to serve him.

Her subordination is thus a *proactive* subordination. It is a vocation which she takes into her own hands, so to speak, and pursues with every fiber of her being. It is not passive subservience but active engagement. Hence its application, far from being restricted to isolated occasions, represents the prevailing, moment-by-moment pattern of her relationship with the Lord.

When applied to marriage, subordination of this kind ennobles the wife. She becomes a creative and energetic partner. She interacts thoughtfully and actively with her husband. She becomes so much more, radically more, than simply a deferential partner in times of dissent. She is also more than a competitor vying for equal status. Confident of her equality to her husband, she passionately uses that equality as a platform for revolutionary action, the sort of action which makes other revolutionaries look insipid by comparison. She throws herself into fulfilling the needs of her husband, viewing his interests as more important than her own (Phil. 2:3).

Revolutionary indeed! What person with even a modicum of self-respect, with even the slightest measure of egalitarian propriety, would dare to subordinate her interests to those of another? We have met just such a person: Jesus Christ. He viewed his position of equality to God as a reason to submit himself to the appalling death of crucifixion. By doing so, he put our interests ahead of his own. He regarded our needs as more important than his own. He "lined up under" us—not in the sense that he became inferior to us, but in the sense that he gave priority to our needs.

Does this kind of self-sacrifice offend our enlightened minds? Does the subordination of Jesus scandalize our egalitarian sensibilities? Of course not! It is gospel, good news, because it is the grounds of our salvation. Through the subordination of the Son of God, we are exalted.

Exaltation by subordination! It is a profound paradox. It is the provocative way of Jesus Christ—and now also the provocative way of wives who have in themselves the same attitude that was in Christ Jesus (Phil. 2:5), who willingly "line up under" their husbands, who view the needs of their husbands as more important than their own, who seek to exalt their partners—and in doing so exalt themselves.

Discerning Eyes

It is possible to go even further in our understanding of subordination. Once again the second chapter of Philippians is illuminating. "Let each of you look not only to his own interests, but also to the interests of others" (2:4). A submissive wife looks out for her husband's interests. She focuses a discerning eye on him. She examines his moods, analyzes his fears, observes his joys, and diagnoses his anxieties.

This is a radical departure from the norm. Usually, we are preoccupied with our own interests. The preponderance of waking hours are typically spent in self-reflection—analyzing our own moods, nurturing our own desires, and pursuing our own agendas. But a wife who subordinates herself to her husband will take her eyes off herself and focus them sharply on her husband. She becomes more interested in him than she is in herself.

In practice this means two things. First of all, wives who embrace the call to subordination will resist the inclination to dominate their husbands. In Genesis 3, we saw that a woman's besetting temptation is to compensate for the ineptitude of her husband by seeking mastery over him. Even good husbands can, by inaction or laziness or insecurity or just poor judgment, drive their wives to frustration, prompting them to take *over* from their husbands, rather than lining up *under* them. The feminine arsenal is filled with a battery of weapons capable of mounting a formidable challenge for the "top position": biting critiques, aggressive action, manipulative moods, sexual blackmail, stubborn silence, nagging criticism. But a godly wife will forsake them all. Rather than push her own agenda, she will seek to honor her husband.

Sympathetic Eyes

This suggests a second application. A submissive wife will take pains to insure that the eye she focuses on her husband is a sympathetic eye. When perplexed by his behavior, she will, instead of engage in condemnation or self-pity, stop and ask herself searching questions. Why is he slow to respond to my requests? Why does he come home and turn on the television or surf the Internet instead of talking to me? Why does he keep his feelings to himself? Why does he get angry and snap so quickly? Why does he seldom express gratitude for my labors on his behalf? Why is he more interested in his male friends? Why does he spend money on foolish things? Why does he not listen to my advice? Why is he plagued by stress and anxiety? Why is he so easily threatened? Why is he insecure? Why can't he break out of his irritating habits? Why does he treat other women with greater interest than he treats me? Why is he so negative? Why does he seldom come home on time? Why does he always expect me to mesh with his schedule? Why does he rarely say he loves me—and when he does, why is it so unconvincing?

Too often we permit questions like these to pass without sympathetic examination. It is always easier to allow frustrations to fester and to explode in verbal criticism than to do the difficult work of drawing a bead on the mind of the husband. Focusing a sympathetic eye on the husband is the way of subordination. It is also the way of healing, both for a weary wife and for her husband.

Praying Hearts

But just because a wife asks the right questions does not mean she will find correct answers. Careful observation does not guarantee accurate analysis. The latter is won only by supernatural assistance. The process of focusing her sights on the husband must be bathed in prayer. Questions such as the ones asked above ought to be addressed not in the first instance to female confidants or to marriage counselors or even to the spouse himself, but to an all-knowing God. To the Lord she must turn with questions and plead for supernatural insight into her husband. And she will receive a response: to prayerful hearts come illuminating answers.

With the assurance of a divine response, why do wives pray so infrequently for their husbands? Is it because they are predisposed not to pray? Earnest prayer does not come naturally to any of us. And it is certainly torture to our adversary the Devil; he will do anything in his considerable power to thwart a wife's prayer on behalf of her husband. The very tendency to neglect prayer ought itself to become the object of our prayers. We must pray that we would pray—and in particular, pray for husbands.

It would be tempting to suggest examples of the possible insights flooding the mind of a wife who inquires prayerfully into the ways of her husband—tempting, but not necessarily beneficial. Every husband is different, and examples pertinent to one might be irrelevant to another. Moreover, the provision of examples might cause wives to neglect the hard work of drawing a bead on their own husband. And it is the hard work that the Lord rewards.

But for purposes of illustration, I will venture one example. It may be that after earnest and prayerful inquiry a wife discovers that her husband derives a large portion of his identity from the level of material success he can strain from a fickle marketplace. As a result, it dawns on her that he needs her unconditional acceptance irrespective of his economic productivity, the size of his salary, or the standard of his living—matters which foster in him an acute sense of inferiority. With fresh insight into her husband's heart, a proactive wife will seek to inundate her husband with unmerited encouragement. In this way, submission to her husband moves beyond prayerful inquiry and blossoms into a resolve to do whatever it takes to minister to him at the level of his need.

That is the pattern of Christ. Looking down from heaven, he inquired into the needs of human hearts. Turning his sights onto our shriveled souls, he identified a debilitating defect. Mercifully, he took the next step and met us at our point of need; leaving the glory of heaven, he submitted to the brutalities of a cross. He walked the path of subordination and now bids us to do the same.

A RADICAL WIFE AND HER RESOURCES

How is it humanly possible to be so devoted to the needs of another? We are capable of only so much sacrifice. At some point, even the most self-giving wife reaches a limit. Fully spent, she collapses in exhaustion and despair.

While there is doubtless a limit to what humans can venture on behalf of another, biblical subordination is more than a human venture. It is the adventure of three persons—a wife, a husband, and the Lord himself, with the Lord supplying the resources for the partnership. On their own and by themselves, wives cannot reproduce the subordination of Jesus Christ. But they are neither on their own nor by themselves; drawing on the Lord, wives can drink from an inexhaustible supply of supernatural assistance.

Three rivers in North America provide passage for a seemingly endless volume of water. The frigid Athabasca pushes northward and empties its contents into Great Slave Lake and, via the Mackenzie River, ultimately into the Arctic Ocean. The meandering North Saskatchewan runs placidly to the east and deposits its massive flow into Lake Winnipeg, which empties into Hudson Bay and the North Atlantic. The turbulent Columbia tumbles westward where it seems almost singlehandedly to raise the level of the Pacific Ocean.

Early explorers were astonished when they discovered that all three rivers derived from a single source. What possibly could sustain such a huge flow of water? The answer is the Columbia Icefields, a huge sheet of ice almost two hundred square miles in size and at places over twelve hundred feet deep. Here at the hydracenter of the continent is a glacier capable of sustaining an almost unlimited supply of icy liquid. Yet—and here is the important point—the capacity of this prodigious ice field, even if multiplied by exponents, could never match the volume of the living refreshment God is prepared to pour into our marriages. The capacity of one spouse to give sacrificially to the other is subject to limitless renewal.

Yet many wives look first to their own resources. It is a habit ingrained in them by their independent spirits or by their religious upbringings or by their desires to please their husbands. Wives too often derive their identities on the basis of whether, by their own resources, they can make their husbands happy. Sooner or later they hit a wall. Submission becomes too difficult. When their husbands are insensitive or uncaring or inattentive or harsh, wives begin to lose respect for their partners. Pangs of guilt may push the wives to redouble their efforts at submission, but the results will be the same. "What does it take to please him?" will be the cry of disheartened wives.

Soon wives may even become bitter toward God. The divine injunction to subordinate themselves to their husbands has put them at the whim of uncaring taskmasters. Marriage becomes a grueling trial. The men to whom they vowed submission now only remind them of their failures. They resent their husbands.

This is the sticky web of a legalistic approach to submission, and too often there appears no escape short of throwing in the towel and abandoning the partnership altogether. But divorce is the harshest critic of all and multiplies the guilt still further.

Thankfully, there is a better approach. It is to exchange the *duty* of subordination for a *spirit* of subordination. The former is something a wife ventures on her own, in her own strength, while the latter is a gift of God. Indeed, only the Lord can vanquish the self-reliance that makes subordination seem like an impossible burden, and only the Lord can revive a heart so that it becomes, willingly and proactively, subordinate to the needs of her husband.

To the Lord, then, a wife turns for a spirit of subordination, and when she does she will find that her identity now derives from the Lord. It is the Lord who gives her strength to be what she was created to be. No longer bound to perform a "duty," she is free to serve her husband from a full heart. She is content with Christ. She is complete in Christ. Through Christ she has received a spirit of submission, indeed a mirror image of his own submission. And like Christ, she is exalted.

WHAT IF HUSBANDS ARE ABUSIVE?

When a wife is enabled by the Lord to invest herself proactively in her husband, she runs the risk of being taken for granted by her husband or, worse, of being treated like a doormat—the object of a husband's emotional, and perhaps even physical, abuse. The apostle Paul actually anticipates the possibility. Immediately after encouraging wives to submit to their husbands, he adds an important pastoral qualification: "For the husband is the head of the wife even as Christ is the head of the church, his body, and is himself its Savior. Now as the church submits to Christ, so also wives should submit in everything to their husbands" (Eph. 5:23–24).

The flow of Paul's thought is clear. In an ideal marriage, a husband will be the head of his wife in the same way as Christ exercises headship over the church—by becoming her savior, by pouring himself out on her behalf. To that kind of husband—one who lovingly serves his partner—a wife will submit as eagerly as the church does to Christ.

But what if a husband's love fails to materialize? What if a husband acts not as a nurturing savior but as an abusive demagogue? Must wives still submit? Here it is vital to remember that the biblical injunction—wives submit to your husbands—is not conditional. It is always the privilege of a wife to minister proactively to her husband by seeking to identify and meet his deepest needs. That is the single piece of advice which the apostle gives to wives, and it remains operative even when husbands fail to "save" their wives in the way Christ saves the church.

There is, however, an important caveat. Husbands must *never* mistreat their wives. Spousal abuse, physical or emotional, is an abomination to God. A wife is never called to become the object of the ill temper of her husband. To defer to an abusive husband is *not* biblical submission. It may in fact be to act as an accomplice in his crime.

A truly submissive wife, as we have seen, seeks to minister to her husband according to his best interest. It is never in his best interest to become the object of his abuse. Instead, biblical submission may require a wife—on certain occasions—to create space between herself and her husband, in other words, to bring his abuse to an end by separating herself from him.

The aim of God's Word is always to promote the marital ideal. It seeks to lift our marriages to higher levels. That is why it encourages subordination. When wives are empowered by God to nurture a spirit of subordination, ministering proactively to husbands at the points of their deepest need, the wives will themselves—just like Christ in his submission—be supremely exalted.

REVOLUTIONARY WIVES

A testament to this reality may be found in the marriage of Martin and Katherine Luther. When Martin, a rebellious monk, married Katie, a fugitive nun, he did so to spite the Pope and to affirm his opposition to clerical celibacy. It was not a marriage conceived in love. "I am not infatuated," said Martin of his new bride. But after years of sharing heart and home with a remarkably self-giving woman, Luther was profoundly changed. Later in life and on more than one occasion he confessed to being romantically smitten. "My Katie is in all things so obliging and pleasing to me that I would not exchange my poverty for the riches of Croesus." "The greatest grace of God is when love persists in marriage." "The dearest life is to live with a godly wife." "Katie, you have a husband who loves you. Let someone else be Empress!"[1]

Clearly, it was Katherine's "obliging" and "pleasing" manner, her numerous acts of proactive service, that transformed the marriage into an exalted union. And not just their union. As noted above, four hundred years of German partnerships have drawn encouragement from the model of domestic relations nurtured within the home of Katherine Luther. The subordination of one woman exalted a nation!

It also exalted Katherine. As a wife, she was called to provide a mirror image of the subordination of God's Son. Living in accordance with this call, Katherine was personally fulfilled. Sadly, many women neglect this call and seek fulfillment in self-serving pursuits and as a result fail to experience the paradox of exaltation through subordination.

The possibility of finding ultimate satisfaction in the pursuit of one's own interests is as unlikely as a fish discovering fulfillment outside its bowl. To leap into a world for which it was not created spells doom for the fish. So, too, for human beings.

The social landscape is littered with those who have leaped into the realm of self-interest only to collapse in frustration and disappointment. We must be alert to the same outcome in marriage and fix our eyes on our created purpose. For wives, it means to focus on the self-giving image of God. No woman who has ever done so—whether she be Katherine Luther or anyone else—has failed to be deeply satisfied by being highly exalted.

We began by acknowledging that the imperative, "wives submit to your husbands," can sound harsh and objectionable to contemporary ears. After close inspection, we have discovered that it is more radical than we first thought. It is not, as modern critics might conclude, a call to embrace an inferior status. It is more provocative than that. It represents a call to wives to give to their husbands what belongs to the wives by right. Fully equal to their husbands, godly wives choose to put the needs of their husbands before their own. They *are* not subordinate, but with God's help they *willingly* subordinate themselves.

It is the volitional aspect of subordination that makes it so revolutionary. It is also what makes it so exalting. It was the willing submission of Jesus that paved the way for the power of heaven to invade what would otherwise have been the unremarkable existence of a Galilean carpenter. The humility of Jesus unto death precipitated an outpouring of blessing that continues to this day.

The same thing happens in marriage. When a wife embraces the one piece of marital advice directed to her, when she willingly and proactively subordinates herself to her husband, the power of God springs to action and transforms her marriage into a union that blesses not only her personally but also everyone who comes into contact with it.

Women eager to shape their worlds will not find the levers of power in the domineering attitudes so often associated with the opposite gender—the egotistical attitudes by which men vainly seek to produce something of lasting good—but rather in the pattern of the One who alone is able to transform the human condition: in short, by exhibiting in their marriages the radical spirit of Jesus Christ. It is the spirit of subordination. It is also, paradoxically, the way of exaltation. And it is the way by which the world is shaped for the good.

In closing, it may be helpful to meditate on words written long ago in tribute to a wife's proactive subordination. Unfortunately, some would say, the words are written by a man. Happily, others might respond, they were inserted into the man's biography by his wife—a wife who seemed to celebrate every memory of her husband. Indeed, Susannah Spurgeon gave highest praise to her husband Charles: "You were the most tender, gracious and indulgent of husbands."[2] Here, in the words of Charles, is a portrait of the exalted submission of Susannah:

> She delights in her husband, in his person, his character, his affection; to her, he is not only the chief and foremost of mankind, but in her eyes he is all-in-all; her heart's love belongs to him, and to him only. She finds sweetest content and solace in his company, his fellowship, his fondness. . . . At any time, she would gladly lay aside her own pleasure to find it doubled in gratifying him. She is glad to sink her individuality in his. . . . She asks not how her behavior may please a stranger, or how another's judgment may approve her conduct; let her beloved be content, and she is glad.[3]

6

A HUSBAND'S LOVE

The man who thoroughly loves God . . . is the only man who will
love a woman ideally—who can love her with the love God thought
of between them when he made man male and female. The man, I
repeat, who loves God with his very life . . . is the man who alone
is capable of grand, perfect, glorious love to any woman.

GEORGE MACDONALD

We have discovered a fascinating bit of trivia in our examination
of biblical marriage. Of all the advice the apostle Paul could have
offered in support of strong marriages, he limits himself to a
single word to each spouse. A wife should *submit* to her husband
and a husband should *love* his wife. Board-game trivia it may
seem, but the twofold counsel is anything but trivial. Indeed,
it comes with a remarkable guarantee. If both partners fulfill
their respective word in marriage and do so simultaneously, they
will enjoy a union that reflects the breathtaking glory of God
himself.

A RADICAL VIEW OF RELATIONSHIPS

Before turning the magnifying glass on the injunction for the husband, it will be helpful to note Paul's unique perspective on a variety
of social relationships. In his letter to the Ephesians, he constructs
three sets of parallel couplets to underscore the roles not only of
wives and husbands, but also of parents and children and of employers and employees:

Wives	submit to your husbands	5:22
Husbands	love your wives	5:25
Children	obey your parents	6:1
Fathers	do not exasperate your children	6:4
Slaves	obey your earthly masters	6:5
Masters	treat your slaves in the same way	6:9

It is immediately noticeable that each of these couplets describes a relationship in which reciprocal responsibilities are required. The wife has a responsibility to her husband. So, too, does the husband to his wife. Similarly with children and parents, slaves and masters—each has a responsibility to the other.

The emphasis of Paul on the reciprocal nature of these relationships would have evoked a mixed response from his first-century readers. Few would have blinked at the responsibility Paul assigns to the first party of each relationship. It was expected for wives, children, and slaves to defer to their "overseers." But to suggest that a reciprocal responsibility was owed by husbands, fathers, and masters would have broken new and radical ground in the matrix of social relations.

Marriage, in particular, was viewed as a one-way street, and the husband held the right of way. In both Greco-Roman and Jewish societies, wives were meant to dance in attendance to their husbands. Only the husband could terminate a marriage, and he could do so at will. As Rabbi Jesus ben Sirach put it: "If she does not go as you direct, separate yourself from her."[1] Against this backdrop, the perspective advanced by the apostle Paul is unconventional. It is no longer just the behavior of wives that is held up to scrutiny. Husbands, too, have responsibilities. They are obliged to protect not just their own rights but the rights of their wives as well.

SUPERNATURAL LOVE

According to Paul, it is the right of the wife to receive and the responsibility of a husband to provide love. "Husbands, love your wives" (Eph. 5:25). Few men will rebel at this command. Most husbands aspire to love their wives. Yet seldom has there been a word susceptible to a wider variety of interpretations. Modern clichés about love demonstrate the point: "Peace and love," "All you need is love," "Let's make love." In the first colloquialism, love represents an antidote to violence; in the second, a vision of utopian bliss; in the last, a desire for sexual intercourse. The wide range of meaning attributed to the term *love* is enough to tax even the most gifted lexicologist.

What does biblical love actually mean? Fortunately, the apostle Paul leaves us in little doubt of what he means by the term. Just as he explained the subordination of a wife by using a qualifying *as* clause, so he also expounds the nature of a husband's love with a similar clause. "Husbands, love your wives, *as Christ loved the church and gave himself up for her*" (Eph. 5:25). The twelve words of this *as* clause require close examination. There is scarcely a more potent assembly of words in the entire Bible, and by them Paul provides a crisp and profound definition of love.

The first and most obvious feature of the clause is that Christ is presented as the exemplar of love and the church as its recipient: "Husbands, love your wives, as Christ loved the church [when he] gave himself up for her." The verb used to describe the extent of Christ's love is the Greek term *paradidomi*, which may be translated "he gave himself over for." It is a technical term in the writings of Paul for the most radical demonstration of self-abandonment in history—the sacrificial death of Christ on the cross. By allowing his lifeblood to be drained out on a Roman gibbet, Christ proved himself to be the archetype of self-emptying love.

What mortal can understand a love so extraordinary? Not even, it seems, the apostle Paul. Earlier in the same epistle to the Ephesians, Paul concludes that it is impossible to comprehend, in full measure, the infinite dimensions of Christ's love. It is simply too broad, too long, too high, and too deep. It is a love that "surpasses knowledge" (3:18–19).

There is, however, an exercise we can perform to derive a more precise understanding of this love. We must picture in our minds the outer limits of Christ's sacrifice, the two points forming the launching pad and the destination of his love. Heaven, certainly, represents the point of departure. If we could imagine the incomparable splendor that surrounded Jesus in heaven, we could appreciate how much love was required to pry him loose from such eternal bliss. The cross, on the other hand, was love's destination. If we could imagine the appalling nature of crucifixion, we could gain an appreciation of the depth of love required to embrace a fate so brutal. The reality, of course, is that none of us can fully comprehend either the splendor of heaven or the horror of a cross. They represent polar extremes and encompass a gulf infinitely wide. But it is precisely that gulf that represents the measure of Christ's love.

This dramatic insight underscores a point which has recurred frequently in our journey through biblical passages on marriage. The marital ideal is pitched at a very high level. Christ, and his example of infinite love, is beyond the capacity of finite minds to comprehend. But if we cannot comprehend this love, how can we ever achieve it? With the standard set so high, what hope do we have of reaching the marital summit? None, if left to our own efforts and power; but much in every way if we turn to our Guide for supernatural help.

Marriage requires a miracle, indeed a succession of miracles. Husbands, especially, must reckon humbly with this truth. They must acknowledge that left to their native devices they will never be able fully to grasp—let alone achieve—the measureless love that is meant to inundate their marriages, the matchless love of the crucified Christ. For this reason, they must seek prayerfully the enlightenment that only God can provide. Husbands must implore the Lord for greater access to the mysteries of the love of Christ.

The enormity of Christ's love suggests an important implication for marriage. A husband must come to view his love as *much more than a reciprocal duty*. His love was never meant to be a mere response to his wife's subordination. Husbands do not offer their love only when they feel their wives deserve it. That was not the way with Christ. He poured his love into us when we least deserved it. It was when we were most unattractive, "while we were still sinners, [that] Christ died for us" (Rom. 5:8). True love always and aggressively takes the initiative, flowing unconditionally into the hearts of those who may not merit it.

The radical nature of Christ's love is missed by men who make a habit of pointing out to their wives the importance of submission. Husbands who track closely evidence of their wives' subordination invariably neglect their own responsibility. The call of a husband to love his wife ought to be so all-consuming that a husband has little time to attend to his wife's submission.

What does the biblical love of a husband look like in practice? Once again, the model is Jesus Christ. We can identify six salient features of the love of Christ. The first two may be framed in terms of prohibitions (what his love is not) and the last four in terms of affirmations (what it is).

Never Unfaithful

First of all, a husband's love is *never unfaithful*. The love of Christ for the church is extremely possessive ("I know my own" [John 10:14]), fiercely protective ("No one will snatch them out of my hand" [John 10:28]), intensely devoted ("If anyone enters by me, he will be saved" [John 10:9]), and radically sacrificial (I lay down my life for the sheep [John 10:11]). Nothing could ever prompt the Lord to spread his affections among those who do not belong to him ("I came that *they* may have life and have it abundantly" [John 10:10]).

And love like this evokes a response in kind: the people of God return an all-encompassing love. They love God with *all* their heart, with *all* their soul, and with *all* their might (Deut. 6:5). The fidelity of a loving God engenders loyalty in his subjects, begetting reciprocal responses of love (see Deut. 5:7).

The same pattern applies in marriage. When husbands demonstrate unwavering faithfulness to their wives, they prompt a response in kind. Their women will be devoted to them. Husbands must guard this fidelity at all costs. They must admit no rivals to their love. A wife should know herself to be the sole recipient of her husband's romantic affection. As he vowed at the altar, a husband must forsake all others.

A wandering eye can be a husband's greatest nemesis, and today, with erotic images bombarding the senses at every turn, it can be an overwhelming adversary. When flames of lust are ignited, when extramarital fantasies are entertained, when sexual purity is threatened, husbands must take quick, aggressive, and even ruthless action to distance themselves from temptation. A casual glance can turn into a prolonged stare. No enticement overwhelms so quickly, damages the human soul so deeply, or undermines good marriages so irreparably. Faithfulness must be cultivated with utmost vigilance.

How is it done? How do we post a vigilant guard when infidelity is marketed on every screen? There is a way. We must nurture, first of all, faithfulness in our relationship with Christ. We must fix our sights on him every day, several times a day, drawing in fresh drafts of spiritual refreshment from the word of Christ, receiving each day anew the love he pours into our unworthy hearts. It is not ultimately biblical warnings against infidelity that sanctify our behavior as much as fresh encounters with the living Christ. Transformed daily by the faithfulness of our Lord, we are supernaturally empowered to exhibit the same faithfulness to our wives.

Never Divorce

Secondly, a loving husband will *never divorce* his wife. Although the Scriptures may provide an exception to this rule (see Matt.19:9), husbands ought to draw their inspiration from the exceptional love of Christ. It is a love that never parts with its object. Neither trouble nor hardship, neither the present nor the future, neither height nor depth, nor anything else in all creation is able to separate us from the love of God that is in Christ Jesus our Lord (Rom. 8:35, 38–39). There will never be sufficient reason for Christ to abandon his bride, the church which bears his name. We are secure in his eternal embrace. It ought to be the same for wives who are loved by their husbands in the same way as Christ loves the church. Marriages may be subjected to severe trials, but they need never break. At the altar a vow was etched in stone—"till death do us part."

Few in antiquity could countenance such a vow. People were accustomed to easy divorce, and it proved a comforting safeguard in the event of bad marriages. When Jesus uttered the famous prohibition against divorce, it sent a collective shudder down the spines of even his most pious listeners. "If such is the case of a man with his wife," demurred his disciples, "it is better not to marry" (Matt. 19:10)! Many today would express a similar reservation. But we must not succumb to a self-seeking outlook that has produced so much pain and dysfunction within marriage. We should rather be open to the words of a compassionate Messiah. His instruction, far from limiting our options and curtailing our happiness, is designed to promote freedom and fulfillment within marriage. It is for our good that he commands us not to divorce.

A member of our church endured for decades the trials of a wife who suffered from mental illness. Thirty-two years of recurring emotional breakdowns rendered her incapable of even the most elementary affection. She rarely initiated a conversation, seldom responded to levity, and never offered the encouragement of sexual love. It was rather just year after year of mostly stony silence.

One day when her husband visited me in the church office I plucked up the courage to ask him how he managed to remain faithful to his wife and why he never contemplated divorce. "I am so blessed!" was his quick reply. "In what way?" I inquired incredulously. He explained: "I believe the Lord brought the two of us together. I figure he chose me out of all the men of the world to take care of her," (at this point he wrapped his middle finger round his index finger to signify unity). "I have asked God ten thousand times to give her a right mind, but he must have wanted to use her struggles to make me a better person."

Deeply moved, I asked in a voice now only a whisper, "How have you made it this far?" His eyes brightened as if to announce an insight whose goodness had been confirmed a hundred times over the years: "In bed every night after I tuck her in, I take her hand in mine and say, 'I love you.' I don't let a day go by without telling her I love her. Then with hands linked together I pray and we go to sleep."

When the fortieth anniversary of this couple arrived, an occasion marked in our church by the presentation of flowers to the two partners, the husband suggested that in their case it would be best to omit any public recognition since he would be attending church by himself. But how could we allow this accomplishment to pass unacknowledged? I responded that we would honor *him*! Embarrassed at the prospect, he nevertheless gave his consent.

When Sunday rolled around, the husband was waiting nervously at the door of my office. With eyes glistening and unable to speak because of emotion, he handed me a two-word note: "She's here!" For some reason his bride had accepted an invitation to church that morning, which every Sunday for decades she had declined.

And so it was that, as a congregation, we were able to raise a genteel applause to a lady and her gentleman, though few understood the significance of the moment or the measure of the accomplishment. Indeed, most were bewildered when no corsage was produced for the wife. Without hesitation, the husband affixed his boutonniere to her dress. Afterward and on his way out of church, the elderly gentlemen leaned over and whispered in my ear, "I am the happiest man in the world!"

How ironic that it is often the pursuit of "happiness" that tempts husbands to entertain thoughts of divorce. But there is no true happiness in that option. It is only when a husband follows the counsel of the Lord, when he forsakes all others and clings faithfully to his wife, and does so irrespective of inevitable marital disappointments, that he discovers a contentment beyond anything the present age has to offer—an abiding and overwhelming joy that only God can provide. Following the commands of the Lord never diminishes marital fulfillment. It always enhances it.

Always Attentive

We can fill out the portrait of a loving husband by adding four positive affirmations. First of all, a husband who models the love of Christ will *notice* his wife. Love pays attention. Of all the things in the universe vying for the Lord's attention, it is especially us, human beings, who became his focus. We became the objects of his keenest observation. As the apostle John memorably notes, "God so loved *the world*, that he gave his only Son" (John 3:16).

The love of husbands ought to be characterized by a razor-sharp focus on their wives. This may be easier in the early days of marriage when romantic embers burn brightly and love-struck husbands hardly notice anything other than their wives. But as time wears on and the initial sparks begin to wane, other things—the demands of work, the passion for sports, the challenge of parenting, the companionship of male friends—can steal away a husband's attention. The result is marital stagnation in which superficial and brief conversations and perfunctory kisses take the place of deeper interaction.

Many husbands fail to detect the deterioration, or they look primarily to their wives to stoke the marital flame. Sticking closely to their appointed routines, husbands busy themselves with their own projects. Wives, wishing to please their husbands, keep growing frustrations under wraps and then, unwittingly, begin to slide into a state of emotional indifference or despair. When the sterility of the relationship finally becomes unendurable, wives will erupt into—what seems to their husbands—a volcano of irrational negativity. At that point, the marriage is seriously imperiled.

But the point need never arrive. A vigilant husband consciously nurtures his first love. He views his wife as his most cherished earthly possession. He pays attention to her. And when he does, he makes a startling discovery. She becomes the great delight of his heart. Her personality, her gifts, and her interests—now carefully noted by the eyes of her partner—become to him a source of endless fascination. The words of Solomon stand like a capstone over his heart: he enjoys life with his wife whom he loves (Eccles. 9:9). Because she knows herself to be his greatest treasure, she is filled with joy and the sparks of the marriage rarely diminish.

Always Understanding

A loving husband will take pains to *understand* his wife. He will notice not only what she says and how she acts, but will also seek reasons underlying those words and behavior. He will probe beneath the surface for the person she is within. That, of course, is a defining feature of Christ's love. He was not content merely to notice from afar but climbed into a human body in order to deal with us on an intimate level. He was "made like his brothers in every respect" in order that he might "sympathize with our weaknesses" (Heb. 2:17; 4:15). In the same way, a husband ought to pursue insight into the thoughts and emotions of his wife. He ought to learn what shapes her dreams and prompts her fears.

Deep understanding will emerge only through creative verbal interaction. Love talks. It asks questions. Jesus constantly inquired of those he loved. "Why are you so afraid?" (Mark 4:40). "Why are you making a commotion and weeping?" (Mark 5:39). So, too, a loving husband will tenderly ask his wife to reveal her heart and, when necessary, help her to do so.

It will hardly be surprising that the greatest obstacle to an outbreak of God's glory within marriage is a breakdown of communication. When dialogue becomes mundane, one-sided, repetitive, tense, or ceases altogether, mutual understanding will be the casualty. A loving husband will guard against the demise of conversation. He will carve out times for sympathetic interaction and, if necessary, structure times into his daily routine. Uninterrupted communication every day helps to build marital cohesion. So, too, does a date night once a week or a quarterly weekend in the mountains or at the beach. Fixing times is the responsibility of a loving husband. Ongoing dialogue is the fruit of his love.

Many wives long for nothing so much as a husband who sees clearly into their hearts. It is always a poignant moment when, in the course of counseling a troubled couple, I ask the husband how well he thinks he understands his wife. The response is often a confident, "Oh, I understand her perfectly, and have from the beginning. She is a very simple person." On hearing these words, the countenance of a wife will sink. How she wishes her husband did understand her. But seldom does he talk to her on a level deep enough, emotional enough, to produce the understandings he claims to possess and she so deeply craves.

The eighteenth-century philosopher and theologian Jonathan Edwards was regarded by critics as a quiet and cerebral man with only modest social skills. But that opinion was never shared in his home. He cultivated an appreciation for the innermost thoughts of his wife, Sarah, as his writings make evident: "She is of a wonderful sweetness, calmness and universal benevolence of mind . . . and [goes] about from place to place, singing . . . and [is] always full of joy and pleasure. . . . She loves to be alone, walking in the fields and groves, and seems to have some One invisible always conversing with her."[2] The depth of his insight was a gift treasured by Sarah. At her husband's death, grief was mingled with gratitude: "What shall I say? A holy and good God has covered us with a dark cloud. . . . [But I] adore his goodness that we had him so long. . . . Oh, what a legacy my husband . . . has left us!"[3]

A husband eager to plumb the innermost feelings of his wife, willing to turn off the television, rise from the Internet, return from work early, or delay a personal project in order to engage thoughtfully with his wife, will reap not only the satisfaction of deeper insight into the one he loves but also the reward of profound gratitude from the one whose life is now more fully known.

Always Sympathetic

Thirdly, a loving husband will seek to *sympathize* with his wife. Sympathy represents a natural progression from the first two positive brushstrokes of Christlike love. The wife who receives her husband's *attention* and *understanding* will ultimately receive his *sympathy*. He will become her staunchest ally—a sensitive companion, a supportive friend, a caring confidant. Such is the hallmark of the love of

Christ. In the incarnation and crucifixion, he sympathized with us deeply. He interposed himself into our situation. He wore our shoes. He walked the same dusty lanes. He experienced our difficulties. He bore our sin. He embraced our lives. He died our death.

For many husbands, sympathy is not a natural attribute. And, ironically, the more a husband thinks he understands his wife, often the less sympathy he expresses. Understanding can breed contempt. When the weaknesses of a wife are exposed, husbands can become judgmental, harsh, critical, or authoritarian. They can disrespect her opinions, belittle her ideas, demean her accomplishments, correct her use of words, and criticize her initiatives—either in subtle ways or sometimes even in front of others. How a husband treats his wife in public is a very telling measure of the authenticity of his love.

True love sympathizes. It rejoices to support another. Here the apostle Paul sets a high standard of instruction: Love is patient and kind; love does not envy or boast; it is not arrogant or rude. It does not insist on its own way; it is not irritable or resentful. . . . Love bears all things, believes all things, hopes all things, endures all things (1 Cor. 13:4–5, 7). Although these words were addressed to all members of the church at Corinth, they could easily be understood as a call specifically to husbands. Insisting on their own way, protecting the sanctity of their own thinking—while it may represent the way of self-regarding men, it is clearly not the way of love. Love relishes the opportunity to defer to the concerns and the needs of a wife.

Nowhere is this clearer than in Christ's love for us, which can, very helpfully, be paraphrased in terms of a husband's love for his wife: Where is the husband who will bring a charge against his wife? Never! The husband will justify her. Who will condemn his wife? Not the husband! He will intercede on her behalf! When a husband is for his wife, who can be against her? (Rom. 8:31, 33–34). A loving husband is his wife's greatest sympathizer, her most ardent champion.

Always Sacrificial

Fourthly, a loving husband will *sacrifice* for his wife. If we were to scan the dictionary for the perfect synonym of biblical love, we could do no better than the pregnant word *sacrifice*. It certainly sums up the pattern inherent in Christ's love. He noticed something was wrong with the human species. He sought to understand the exact nature of our problem. He sympathized with our need, entering personally into our predicament. And then, remarkably, he took love one gigantic leap forward and poured out his very life for us. He "came . . . to give his life a ransom for many" (Mark 10:45). He sacrificed himself on our behalf. This is the supreme calling of husbands. They love their wives "as Christ loved the church [when he] gave himself up for her" (Eph. 5:25), when he sacrificed himself on her behalf.

It ought to be obvious that sacrifice entails more than a simple willingness to put one's life at risk for another. Several years ago a young woman was attacked by a grizzly bear in the backcountry of the Rockies. Her male partner immediately hurled himself at the bruin, yanked vigorously at its grizzled mane, and quickly became himself the object of the animal's fury. When the bear finally sauntered away, the man had given his life for his partner, while she stumbled hysterically back to the trailhead and to relative safety.

The story is legendary for its sacrificial love. Yet the love of a Christian husband ought to be characterized by an even greater degree of sacrifice—more than a life given in death, but a life given in life. A loving husband will lay down his own life by taking up his wife's. He will make her life his life. He will view her life as dearer to him than his own. He will live her life as though it were his own. He will give his life—in life—for hers. He will give her the gift of his life.

This kind of self-denying love is a mystery to most husbands. Few things are deemed worthy of the sacrifice of their lives—work perhaps, or ambitions, or wealth. But a wife?! Men still nurture the idea that wives are essentially there for them—to serve them, to please them, to love them—and not *vice versa*. How often do men forfeit a personal passion for the good of their wives? How many men will put their work on hold to fulfill a wife's dream? How often do husbands assure their wives in a tangible way that apart from God nothing in their lives is even remotely as important as they are? How many wives are confident that their husbands are willing to sacrifice everything for them? This is not the reality of most marriages. We live in a society where men are more likely to nurture their golf swings, or their reputations, than the hearts of their wives.

REWARDS OF CHRISTLIKE LOVE

And that is tragic—not just for wives, but also for husbands. With the biblical injunction of love comes an extraordinary promise. If a husband loves his wife as Christ loves the church, he will—imagine this!—make her holy, cleansing her by the washing with water through the word, and present her to himself in all her radiance, without stain or wrinkle or any other blemish, but holy and blameless (Eph. 5:26–27).

Biblical love transforms a wife. It is the most powerful shaping agent in the world. Love elevates a wife above everything common and defiled, cleanses her from the sullying influences of her past, and transforms her into a radiant person. It bathes her in the glory of God and removes—from the eyes of her husband and, consequently, from her own eyes too—any taint or blemish. What an exquisite creature is the woman loved by her husband! Men take note. The wife of your dreams—indeed a wife exceeding your dreams—awaits the demonstration in and through you of Christlike love.

Too many husbands adopt a different pattern. They nurture a vision of the ideal woman and then point out to their wives areas where they fall short. They chip away at their wives, often issuing toxic barbs: "Why aren't you more disciplined?" "Why are you putting on weight?" "Why don't you pay more attention to my interests?" "Why are you always late?" "Why is the house a mess?" "Why are the children misbehaving?"

Husbands fail to realize the damaging consequences of this approach. Far from encouraging changes for the better, their words engender bitterness and resentment. In time, wives become demoralized, self-protective, and combative. After years of dispensing verbal criticism, husbands awaken to find themselves in the company of henpecking wives and wonder, with shameless temerity, how it could have happened. The answer is simple: the hen has come home to roost!

There is not the slightest hint of bitterness in true love. "Husbands, love your wives, and do not be harsh with them," instructs the apostle Paul in his letter to the Colossians (3:19). Harshness, bitterness, criticism—each of these dims the radiance of a wife. But love patterned after Christ, a love that adopts the wife's life as though it were its own and makes whatever sacrifices are necessary to promote her best interests, will cause the marital union to explode with the glory of God.

Years ago a friend of mine was preparing to marry a woman with a checkered past and an abrasive personality. She was strong willed, cantankerous, and seemingly ill suited for a partnership which might otherwise, because of the gifts of my friend, climb to impressive heights. Early in their courtship, I mustered the courage to relay to him my concerns about his choice of mate. My friend listened respectfully and then responded with simple words, "But I love her." At the time, it sounded like sentimental drivel. I wondered why he failed to reckon seriously with my concerns. Over the years, the words "But I love her" have been translated into a work of remarkable glory. A later rendezvous with the couple revealed a wife whose character was still strong but now tempered by gentleness and kindness. A bit of heaven appeared on her face. How did it happen? Clearly, she had been transformed by the daily gift of her husband's love.

Men have been talking for centuries about changing society for the better and have poured a vast amount of energy into the endeavor. The result has been an explosion in technology, a proliferation of fast-food outlets, a steady flow of peace treaties, and a multiplication of software packages capable of providing for every human need under the sun. But, sadly, there is little improvement in the quality of our lives. Few people speak optimistically about the future. Cynicism abounds.

In the forty-eight hours before typing out these words, I had chance encounters with four disconsolate men. One was an executive with a high-paying position who was tormented by guilt over the collapse of his thirty-year marriage. Another was an engineer whose car was discovered abandoned on a wilderness road with his wallet and keys neatly packed in the trunk, and whose despair over a failed marriage had left acquaintances fearing the worst. Still another was a security guard whose relish for his new job was tempered by the sadness he now feels about the sixteen hours by road which separate him from a wife with whom he is presently estranged. The fourth is a successful lawyer who shares his bed with a female companion and speaks of the relationship with all the enthusiasm of one who believes that romance always produces more pain than pleasure. If we add to these four the great numbers of men whose marriages are mired in a strained coexistence, who continue to search, often outside matrimony, for a personal connection that will nurture their souls at the deepest level, then we most certainly have identified one of the most tragic statistics of our struggling society—the rudderless male.

But the problem has, as we have seen, a triumphant solution. Sadly, too few take advantage of it. Neither the pundit in the media nor the scholar in the university nor the social worker in government has raised an audible voice in support of the one thing which an apostle from an earlier era prescribed as the most important antidote to the social ills of the world—"Husbands, love your wives." These four words, if applied with resolve, will nurture a woman at the deepest level, with the inevitable result that husbands themselves will bask in the joys of marital contentment.

Why, then, do so few heed Paul's advice? Why is there a reticence to embrace this cure? After all, the apostle reasons with impeccable logic; no one ever hated his own body. He who loves his wife loves *himself* (Eph. 5:28–29). A bit of heaven in the home—who will resist that? And with the glory of heaven invading marriages, hope is renewed for society. Surely such love deserves our attention. Below, we will give closer attention to the glory of a marriage in which the love of a husband has been fully given.

SUBMISSION AND LOVE—WHAT'S THE DIFFERENCE?

First, we must take our analysis of Paul's two words for marriage a step farther. The dual counsel the apostle offers to couples, one word each to the wife and to the husband, would seem at first glance to amount to much the same thing. Both a wife's subordination and a husband's love can be understood in terms of identifying the needs of the other and then venturing every personal resource to meet those needs. In short, both words can be reduced to the idea of sacrificing one's own interests for the good of the other.

Yet there is a sense in which the words are distinct. In particular, both represent in their own ways a reversal of the two maladies that have pummeled the sexes from the beginning. When the first pair consumed the forbidden fruit, they were drawn into a cauldron of intergender conflict. The man began to use the woman, and the woman sought to master the man. This clash has poisoned every marriage ever since and has undermined societies founded on the unions of men and women.

But in the death of Jesus Christ, the self-centeredness of both genders is dealt a mortal blow. In the resurrection of Jesus Christ, a new self-emptying person is miraculously born in everyone in whom Christ dwells (2 Cor. 5:14–17). This new person is the hope of marriage. In husbands, it is a person who no longer seeks to use his wife but to love her by laying down his life and picking up hers. In wives, it is a person who no longer seeks to master her husband but proactively works to serve him at his point of need. The two partners are the exact opposites of their primordial selves, and in them the bitter consequences of the fall are reversed. Marriages become populated by mutually self-giving partners—they do, that is, if both husbands and wives are "in Christ," if both have received by faith the miracle of new birth which Jesus died and rose to provide.

There is another sense in which the roles of marriage differ. Love takes the initiative and submission responds to that initiative. Paul illustrates the difference by contrasting the roles of Christ and the church. Love is something Christ initiated ("Christ is the head of the church, his body, and is himself its Savior" [Eph. 5:23]). Submission is the church's response ("Now . . . the church submits to Christ" [Eph. 5:24]). The pattern is meant to be duplicated in marriage. The husband leads out with Christlike love. The wife responds with church-like submission.

Every year, once a year, thousands of spectators line the banks of the river Thames in London and await anxiously the crackling discharge of an ancient cannon. The deafening blast signals the start of what is arguably Britain's greatest sporting spectacle, the nearly two-century-old tradition called "The Boat Race." Eight-person crews from Cambridge and Oxford strain oar against oar to be the first to cross underneath Hammersmith Bridge, the finish line of the famous regatta.

Trained eyes always look for an early advantage; in particular, they focus on the oarsman occupying the first seat in each boat, the position known as "the stroke." The person sitting there is responsible for setting the pace of those rowing behind. As the stroke goes, so goes the entire boat. It is a thing of beauty to watch crews working together, the stroke setting the pace, the others responding in kind. It is a labor of exquisite harmony in quest of the esteemed silver cup.

Marriage requires a similar harmony. The husband, occupying the position of the stroke, initiates the pace. The wife–a rower every bit his equal–responds with matching oar. Husband and wife work together, fulfilling the responsibility of their respective seats. Love and subordination labor in unison, collaborating in marital harmony.

It begins with the husband. When he sets the pace with a stroke of cruciform love, his wife responds in kind, and the marital boat moves forward to claim the most coveted victory of all–the prize of reflecting within marriage the glory of God.

Husbands . . . let's love our wives!

BECOMING ONE FLESH

Happy woman and happy man! If heaven be found on earth, they have it! . . . The two are so blended, so engrafted on one stem. . . . So happy a union of will, sentiment, thought, and heart exists between them, that the two streams of their life have washed away the dividing bank, and run on as one broad current of united existence till their common joy falls into the ocean of eternal felicity.

CHARLES SPURGEON

Icy winds lashed at the upper reaches of Everest, gaining in ferocity just as a relatively inexperienced climbing party made its final push to the summit. It was the 10th of May, 1996. By the end of the day, four of the six adventurers would lay entombed at the top of the world, never again to smell a rose or kiss a baby.

It was one of the most tragic chapters in the annals of Himalayan mountaineering and naturally elicited a rash of inquiries. Did the final ascent come too late in the day? Was the grim forecast dismissed too casually? Did the rarefied air blunt human judgment? Each of these concerns was doubtless a factor. Yet in the minds of veteran climbers there was a more sinister impairment. The expedition lacked unity. Disrupted by selfish ambition and rugged individualism, the party splintered into isolated units and negotiated the last gale-battered pitch without the encouragement of mutual support.

Disunity can undermine any human enterprise. But no relationship is more vulnerable to its destructive power than marriage. Between husbands and wives, even the faintest hint of disunity can mushroom into a raging storm. Trivial disagreements, testy traits, minor misunderstandings—irritants which pose little threat to casual friendships can within marriage become icy gales penetrating every corner of the relationship. Helpless to stem the malign winds, many couples tolerate disunity as an unavoidable curse on their relationship and resign themselves to calloused indifference.

What a far cry from the ideal! How can we rise above this kind of division and regain the high ground of marital oneness? Is there an antidote to the winds of disunity?

Absolutely! It comes to us from the hand of God. The Master Physician scribbles a prescription, not on shiny labels stuck to plastic vials, but on leaves of parchment known to us as the Holy Scriptures. Listen to the biblical antidote to marital disharmony: "A man shall leave his father and his mother and hold fast to his wife, and they shall become *one flesh*" (Gen. 2:24). The cure for disunity is summed up by two scintillating words—"one flesh"!

THE MIRACLE OF ONE FLESH

We seldom seek to plumb the riches of this term, often regarding it as a self-evident metaphor. In marriage, two lives converge. They become one flesh. It's as simple as that! Yet the expression "one flesh" cannot be so easily negotiated. If nothing else, it suggests a perplexing mathematical equation in which one plus one equals one. How can that be? Many struggling romantics would pay dearly for an answer. We shall discover that embedded in these two words is a miracle of unspeakable beauty. To mine its riches, we must solve the riddle: What does it mean to be "one flesh"?

In the Bible, the word *flesh* is used to describe what a person is at the core of his or her being. Hence when two people become one flesh, they unite at the deepest level. They become, as it were, ontologically one. Such a dramatic union represents far more than the sum of shared interests or the bond of sexual intimacy. It is a fusion of souls, an organic commingling of two individual lives.

What does it look like in practice? Helpful clues have been deposited in three biblical passages where the term *one flesh* appears. In Genesis 2 we read: "A man shall leave his father and his mother and hold fast to his wife, and they shall become *one flesh*" (v. 24). The next verse helps to unravel the meaning of one flesh: "The man and his wife were both naked and were not ashamed" (v. 25). The two partners, it seems, were unaware of their individual nakedness. Perhaps it was because they were so focused on each other that they were unconscious of their autonomous selves. How can there be shame where there is no self-consciousness? Instead, they were lost in the unblushing joy of attentiveness to the needs of the other.

This suggests a dramatic insight: when two selfless lines of focus intersect, somewhere between the husband and the wife, a brand new entity begins to emerge in which two people actually become one person, the glowing result of the self-giving compassion of both parties. Does this sound mysterious? It should! According to Paul, the drama of one flesh is a profound mystery (Eph. 5:32).

But it is a mystery to which further insights may be added. In a second biblical passage where the term *one flesh* appears, we read the following from the lips of Jesus: "'A man shall leave his father and his mother and hold fast to his wife, and the two shall become one flesh.' *So they are no longer two but one flesh*" (Matt. 19:5–6). The second sentence points to a dynamic reorganization within marriage. Husbands and wives are no longer two apart but one together. Like the fusion of a sperm and an egg, they become a new organism. The fusion does not dissolve their original personalities but redirects those personalities toward each other in such a way that the best traits of each spill out into the other.

A good analogy of this mutual enrichment is the confluence of two rivers, where the volume of each body of water empties into the other and produces one new and mighty torrent far more fertile and navigable than had the two never intersected. Like the merger of the Athabasca and Miette rivers in northern Canada, the one glacier fed and murky and the other spring generated and clear—coming together, their contents commingle and generate a brand new river of novel hues and enlarged capacity. No longer two apart, they are one together.

According to Jesus, the merger of a husband and a wife is the work of God himself. It is something "God has joined together" and therefore something that no man can separate (Matt. 19:6). Who else could take two personalities and conflate them into a single being, prompting them to empty themselves selflessly into the other, creating in the process a brand new being more radiant and useful than had the two remained individually apart? It is a work of God.

The final passage in which the term *one flesh* is used may be the most illuminating of all. "A man shall leave his father and mother and hold fast to his wife, and the two shall become one flesh. This mystery is profound, and I am saying that it refers to Christ and the church" (Eph. 5:31–32). Here Paul draws a comparison between husbands and wives and Christ and the church, and then explains why the second relationship, between Christ and the church, is such a fruitful union. It is because Christ "nourishes and cherishes" his people, because he lavishes his compassion on them, because he gives himself up in death to make them "members of his body" (Eph. 5:29–30), because he draws the church into himself by pouring himself into the church.

At first thought, the work of Christ defies imagination. How can an outward thrust, such as outpouring love, serve to draw anything in? Such a massive outflow ought to push away, not attract. But there is something special about the love of Christ. The more it surges outward the more it pulls in. And when husbands and wives embody this love, when they "nourish and cherish" each other in the same way as Christ does the church, they will draw each other into themselves and create a bond so tight that nothing but death can sever it. Self-giving love is the catalyst of oneness of flesh.

POURING OUT AND DRAWING IN

It is worth reviewing what we have discovered in the three biblical passages above. The notion of one flesh signifies something more than the merger of two lives emotionally or physically. It represents the creation of a new being in which two people pour so much of themselves into the other that they no longer are two apart but one together.

It is like two glasses, each full of water, whose contents are emptied into the other. When each is emptied simultaneously, a third glass is required to capture all the refreshment. That third and larger glass, now topped up to the brim with water from the other two, stands in place of the other two. This is what happens in marriage: two distinct people become one flesh. The more fully a husband and a wife pour themselves into each other, the more surely they draw each other into themselves, creating in the process a new and more vibrant being. Just as Christ's own self-giving love serves to unite men and women to himself in an explosive new body called the church, so, too, the love of a husband and a wife will create a dynamic new being called one flesh.

Have you ever witnessed one flesh in action? It is one of the great wonders of creation. When a husband redirects the river of his passions—a river which normally would flow in the direction of his own ambitions and projects—into the interests of his wife, when he takes up her life and begins to live it as though it were his own, when he cancels a trip or an appointment or a sporting engagement in order to commit more time to fulfilling her needs, when he sits down after a busy day and initiates a conversation that truly taps into her heart, when he responds to her criticisms by gathering her tenderly into his arms—how can this not but draw in a wife!

And when a wife pours herself into the things that interest her husband, serving him at the point of his needs, redirecting the flow of her life to insure that he is receiving maximum refreshment, asking not whether he is ministering to her but only whether she is emptying her resources fully into him—how can this love not but draw in a husband!

And when both partners pour themselves *simultaneously* into the other, a brand new "community," far more radiant and fruitful than just the sum of the two individuals, is miraculously created.

ONENESS IN THE TRIUNITY OF GOD

Now we are ready for the most amazing discovery of all. The surge of love which unites husbands and wives in the remarkable bond called one flesh is something that originates within the triune God. Father, Son, and Holy Spirit are three distinct persons yet one perfectly united Being, and represent the most dynamic fusion in the universe.

What sustains the tri-union? According to the Holy Scriptures, it is the miracle of self-giving love.

The trait is featured repeatedly in the gospel of John, where we read that the Father loves the Son (John 15:9; 17:23, 24, 26), and the Son loves the Father (John 15:9), and the Holy Spirit glorifies the Father and the Son (John 14:26), and the Son glorifies the Father (John 17:4), and the Father glorifies the Son (John 17:1). Each member of the Godhead, in a perpetual flow of boundless affection, lavishes himself on each of the others such that what belongs to one belongs to the others. In the words of the Son: "All that the Father has is mine" (John 16:15) and "all mine [are his]" (John 17:10). Has there ever been such an unrestrained, extravagant, spectacularly self-emptying display of love as that which occurs in the Godhead?

The stunning answer is—yes! Such a love ought to characterize the bond of husbands and wives. It was the Creator's intention to stamp the marital union with his triune imprint. "God created man in his own image . . . male and female he created them" (Gen. 1:27). Husbands and wives together imaging God, reproducing in their relationship the same self-emptying love that characterizes the Trinity. Marriage could scarcely be more replete with significance. Husbands and wives—reflecting together the glory of the love of God!

Do we understand the extraordinary radiance of this partnership? The apostle Paul prays we would "know the love of Christ that surpasses knowledge" so that we would "be filled with all the fullness of God" (Eph. 3:19), so that we will be vessels brimming over with a torrent of God's infinite love, channeling its overflow into the person closest to you. In marriage, that person is our spouse. He or she becomes the recipient, through us, of a tidal wave of divine love.

This is God's plan for marriage: a husband and a wife funneling into each other a surfeit of heavenly refreshment, replicating between them the love that binds the Trinity itself. It is the most sublime display of oneness.

Does such an exalted union sound unrealistic? How many couples actually exhibit Trinitarian love? Isn't the sobering reality much less impressive? Doesn't the germ of selfishness invade every marriage? Where is the couple that doesn't fall well short of the miracle of triune love?

Even if the answers to these questions are discouraging, we must not recoil from the biblical ideal any more than we should recoil from the adventure of flying simply because on occasion planes do not land safely. The husband and the wife who push on to the marital summit will make a startling discovery: even when disappointing episodes of selfishness invade their marriage, those disappointments can be used to strengthen the marital bond and lift them to even greater heights.

ONE FLESH IN PRACTICE

Here's how it works. Normally when disunity assaults a marriage, husbands and wives look for psychological solutions. They ask probing questions about the attitudes and circumstances that gave rise to the discord and then seek to diffuse the conflict through therapeutic methods or techniques. These measures can be helpful, but they do not penetrate to the heart of the problem.

At the root, marital disunity is not just a psychological problem but a theological problem. When a relationship is mired in hurt feelings or stony indifference or festering bitterness, it is a signal that selfishness has invaded the union. Wherever selfishness reigns, the love of God is absent. The two cannot coexist. When struggling partners awaken to this reality, they may at first grieve, but they can also, remarkably, rejoice. Grieve that in their selfishness they have fallen short of God's glory, but rejoice that in acknowledging the nature of their problem they are ripe for a solution.

The solution always entails a confession—and according to the Word of God, it is a confession of sin. The word *sin* strikes an ugly (or comic) chord in the ears of many contemporary minds, but it contains a truth with a blessing. It is only when we face our sin honestly that we are ready for deliverance, and deliverance of the most uplifting kind. On the basis of the cross work of Jesus Christ, God grants two priceless gems: forgiveness of sins (Ezek. 36:25; Heb. 10:12) and newness of heart (Ezek. 36:26; Heb. 10:22). The first gem—forgiveness—absolves us of an imperfect past. The second gem—a new heart—prepares us for a God-glorifying future.

By the grace of God in Jesus Christ, divine love flows into the hearts of penitent husbands and wives, and in such enormous quantity that it necessarily spills out into the heart of the other. As a result, the marital bond solidifies. But—and here is a striking reality—this new infilling of love would never have occurred had discord not driven husbands and wives to make a confession of their sin to God. Hence the sin that could have torpedoed the marriage, breaking it into a thousand pieces, is used by God to bring two people closer together. A sovereign God can bend even sin to his purposes.

HOW DISUNITY CAN FOSTER UNITY

This suggests an insight few could have imagined. Disunity can become a launching pad to oneness of flesh. It may sound paradoxical, but it is reassuringly true. Even when the ruts of marital discord are cut painfully deep and partners are locked up in cocoons of frustration and anger, even when animosity festers for days and months and even years and solutions seem nowhere in sight, and even when expectations are dashed repeatedly by the refusal of both partners to amend their ways or relent on their positions—it is then, especially then, that an opportunity for deliverance presents itself. The only question is: Will the opportunity be seized?

It all comes down to humility—husbands and wives acknowledging that, if they are ever to reach the marital summit, they need help from beyond themselves. Humility—few attributes are more important and few more elusive. How does a couple become humble? Discord itself can pave the way. It can open the eyes of both partners to the futility of their own attempts to achieve marital harmony and underscore the importance of dropping to their knees and pleading with God to open up his treasury of transforming love—forgiving their sins, refashioning their hearts, reviving their love, and translating their weaknesses to strength. By his empowering grace, they can be given a new desire to put the interests of the other ahead of their own, and when they do a bond will grow that is deeper and firmer and more beautiful than anything they might have achieved apart from the pains of disunity.

When I meet with a husband and a wife whose marriage is unraveling, I initially feel as discouraged as the two people sitting in front of me. Puzzling over the impasse, I pray for insight, any insight that might reverse the deterioration of a marriage. Often, and quite unexpectedly, a light switches on in my mind: *God* can mend this union. Yes, *he* can. He *alone* can. And I turn to the couple and beg them to believe in the reviving power of God.

When they respond in humility, defensive thoughts and combative words suddenly give way to contrite hearts, and the two begin to ask God for the miracle of healing. "Heavenly Father, do what only you can do: restore this union!" Later, as the couple is drinking in drafts of divine compassion, it occurs to me that it was only when they humbly confessed their sin and sought the restoration of heaven that their union began to take a turn for the better. Despairing of their own abilities, they sought help from God. And God answered.

Disunity, then, can be a springboard to unity. What a thrilling paradox! This means that no couple, no matter how battered by marital failure, should ever relinquish hope. When resentment and bitterness have become chronic and temptation to retreat into a defensive shell becomes almost irresistible, when neither husband nor wife is willing to concede an advantage to the other, when tempers flare and spirits plummet—it is *especially then* that two partners can be on the cusp of victory.

Their eyes begin to look heavenward. Their hearts begin to soften. Prayers are offered. Trickles of divine love begin to seep into their souls. The trickles then become torrents. Husband and wife, for the first time in a long time, begin to channel the love of Christ into each other. A miracle is taking place. Tongues begin to loosen and tender words are spoken, words which only days before—perhaps only moments before—were locked away in a tightly sealed vault. Apologies are offered. Forgiveness is granted. Who was right and who was wrong—it no longer matters. The improbable is taking place.

A new bond is forming and it is tighter and more beautiful than ever before, a bond arising from the ashes of disunity and despair.

Have you experienced the miracle of a resurrected marriage? Have you been guided back to the trail by a merciful God? Have you cried out humbly for the victory only he can provide? Have you pleaded for the gift of divine help? It is a prayer God wants to answer. It is a prayer God will answer. And when he does, your union will become a masterpiece of his glory.

THE WONDER OF ONENESS

In a world limping along in a fog of loveless relationships, where the majority of partnerships succumb to the storms of self-interest, a marriage topped up and overflowing with the love of Christ stands out like a radiant beacon against the darkest night. Nothing is more impressive. And people will notice. They will behold such a marriage with wonder and give praise to God.

Listen to the praise offered by a well-traveled George Whitefield after observing carefully the marriage of Jonathan and Sarah Edwards: "A sweeter couple I have not yet seen. It causes me to renew those prayers, which, for some months, I have put up to God, that He would be pleased to send me a daughter of Abraham to be my wife."[1]

Or imagine my own wonder when reading the Christmas greeting of a friend whose mate had long borne the travails of an incapacitating disease: "My time is taken up with caring for a very courageous wife as she struggles to cope with the ravages of multiple sclerosis. When she feels frustrated because of the time necessary for her care and says, 'I wish you could get back to your own work,' I reply, 'Caring for you *is* my work.' We remain supremely happy together." Yes, supremely happy together—happy in the daily expression of the self-giving love of the Lord, a love which in turn brings happiness to everyone blessed to see it.

Why does true marital love move our hearts so deeply? It is because it awakens memories of the only thing that really nourishes a human heart: divine love. We were made to receive God's love, and we were made to pour it out into others. When we see it happening in marriage—a relationship perfectly suited to the giving and the receiving of divine love—it ministers deeply to our hearts.

The love of God . . . imbibed. The love of God . . . imparted. As human beings, this is our *raison d'être*, and it is the foundation of every good marriage. C. S. Lewis put it well: "When I have learnt to love God better than my earthly dearest, I shall love my earthly dearest better than I do now. In so far as I learn to love my earthly dearest at the expense of God and *instead* of God, I shall . . . not love my earthly dearest at all. When first things are put first, second things are not suppressed but increased."[2] When husbands and wives drink deeply from the well of God's love, they inevitably pour that love into each other. Oneness with God produces oneness with each other.

Does this kind of unity feature in any marriages you know? Does it—if you are married—feature in yours? It can. It is never too late. You can be "remarried" today for the glory of God. Humbly confess to the Lord the self-centeredness of your heart and ask him to fill you with the love of Christ.

Nor is it ever too soon. If you are hoping to marry or have recently become married, bow before the Lord and ask him for the gift of his love and prepare yourself for the miracle of one flesh.

A CONFESSION

Intrusions of disunity are not foreign to my marriage, but by God's grace, some of our greatest blessings have emerged from the sting of discord. When Lesli and I have needed a fresh perspective, we have dropped to our knees and asked God for the mercy and the selflessness only he can give; and he has always responded by opening our eyes to the needs of the other and by filling us with a desire to meet those needs in more caring ways.

Amazed that we should become recipients of so much grace, we cling more tenaciously than ever to the binding power of God's glory, knowing that by this tether we can be raised to peaks more satisfying than any we have climbed before. But—and here is the vital point—the ascent would have been impossible had we not been confronted by setbacks. It was discord that drove us to pray for a fresh infusion of divine love. In weakness, we cried out to God. In strength, he responded. By his grace, we became increasingly one. *Sola deo gloria!*

Not long ago, the little mountain town of Jasper celebrated the seventy-fifth anniversary of the first ascent of Mount Alberta. The peak is known for its forbidding granite face, creating one of the best-guarded summits in the pantheon of mountaineering. With vertical walls rising thousands of feet above the valley floor and with every route to the summit impeded by a steady bombardment of loose debris and rock, it takes a superhuman effort to reach the top.

In 1925, a multinational expedition was assembled with the intent of being the first to make a successful ascent. Late on an August afternoon, a party of four struggled to the midsection of the mountain. There they were confronted by a severe rock outcropping which, forming a ceiling over their heads, halted their progress. The success of the expedition lay in jeopardy.

Suddenly two men, one Swiss and one Japanese, unroped themselves from the others and, with one climbing onto the shoulders of the other, formed a human ladder. Far up the face of a treacherous mountain, angling perilously over the cliff, with knees buckling, torsos swaying, and hands groping desperately for some kind of grip on the loose rock above, the "ladder" finally snapped into place. Almost miraculously, the other two climbers crawled over footholds supplied by the human legs and shoulders of their brave comrades and, on surmounting the overhang, dropped a rope down to the two whose bond had won them the summit.

Two men, separated by an ocean of cultural differences, forged an almost unearthly connection. Their fusion stands out today as one of the great triumphs of modern mountaineering.

The glory of oneness. The oneness of glory. It is even more triumphant at the marital summit!

PART THREE

CLIMBING ALWAYS UPWARD

8

FUSING BODIES

Man survives earthquakes, epidemics, the horrors of disease, and all the agonies of the soul, but for all time his most tormenting tragedy has been, is, and will be—the tragedy of the bedroom.

LEO TOLSTOY

What is more delightful than sex? It is probably the most exhilarating activity known to human beings. No wonder that among our pantheon of postmodern gods, Aphrodite, the mythological goddess of sexual love, reigns supreme. We fill our screens with her enchanting allurements and absorb an endless projection of erotic images and sensual themes. Even so, it must be said we make far too little of sex. In spite of its high profile in contemporary society, sex is something we understand only slightly.

SEX AND THE GLORY OF GOD

Sex is a revelation of the glory of God. The mingling of two bodies, the clutching, the caressing, the quickening pulse, the ultimate fusion—these are the dramatic outward expressions of the inner reality of oneness of flesh, a reality which, as we have seen, traces its origin to the triune God himself. Sexual union is an expression of the glory of God. A supreme tragedy of our day is that so few people understand the deeper meaning of sex and so few profit from its rewards.

The way to recover the glory of sex is to view it in its original context. At the root, sex is for marriage and marriage is for sex. Recently a friend of mine spoke in honor of his parents-in-law on the occasion of their fiftieth wedding anniversary. He gave the following tribute: "Your persistent recognition of the importance of physical intimacy within marriage has been a role model to countless couples." Then he added a sobering observation: "It is ironic that in a sex-filled culture, marriage isn't where physical intimacy tends to flourish."

Study after study confirms the point: sex abounds in almost every sphere but marriage. This is disturbing, especially for Christians whose founding document, the Holy Scriptures, makes an unmistakable connection between the glory of sex and unity of marriage. My friend's final lament was especially disconcerting: "Among Christians, confusion related to sex is epidemic." When dysfunction invades even the bedrooms of Christians, we know the problem is grave.

EPIDEMIC SEXUAL CONFUSION

It is vital to understand the cause of the problem. For many years, modernity has instructed us that sex is a mere natural phenomenon, an instinct hardwired into our genes for the purpose of propelling our DNA into the next generation. The sexual impulse is the engine that drives the evolutionary process and is therefore a power that cannot be resisted. Just as our appetite for food causes us to consume dead plants and animals, so our appetite for sex drives us to copulate with members of our own species. And so we embrace, perhaps unwittingly, the mantra of scientific naturalism: trust your appetites, pursue them with vigor, and fret not about the consequences. But it is precisely the unrestrained pursuit of natural impulses that causes so much confusion about sex.

The reason is obvious. There is dissonance between the philosophy of naturalism and practical reality. While it may feel natural to give free vent to sexual impulses, it is extremely destructive in practice. Unregulated sex exacts a terrible toll on human lives. It causes alarming pathologies: emotional trauma, unwanted pregnancies, eviscerating guilt, and harmful disease. Nor are these pathologies merely a modern phenomenon. Many were prominent in ancient society as well. As we page through the Bible, we discover that sexual behavior is the subject of frequent analysis, and nowhere more probing than from the quill of a first-century lawyer named Paul. For his insight into the complexities of sex we must turn to his first letter to the church in Corinth.

SEX IN FIRST-CENTURY CORINTH

Even more than most of our modern cities, ancient Corinth was a place of unfettered eroticism. Favorinus, a first-century orator, described Corinth as "a city of Aphroditic-type pleasure beyond all that are or ever have been."[1] No doubt a high percentage of the population engaged in promiscuous sexual behavior. It would take a bold man to suggest that people should do otherwise. But Paul was not given to temerity. When he became convinced that a certain kind of behavior diminished the glory of God and caused great psychological harm to its participants, he could stand against the most entrenched social customs.

Nothing was more congenial to contemporary minds than easy sex. Far from intimidating Paul, it emboldened him. He took aim and—with love in his heart—fired.

The Dangers of Temporary Gratification

In the sixth chapter of his first letter to the Corinthians, Paul goes on the offensive by reciting a well-known maxim of the day, "All things are lawful for me." In other words, he is free to do whatever he wishes so long as it does not conflict with a second maxim—"but not all things are helpful" (1 Cor. 6:12). While most behavior is permissible, not all is beneficial. So the apostle Paul adds an important qualification, "I will not be enslaved by anything." Certain activities, while not forbidden, may be enslaving. If indulging in a particular activity becomes enslaving—that is to say, addicting—it must be avoided.

By announcing this principle, Paul makes a firm break from the free-wheeling spirit of his age and subjects his own behavior to careful guidelines. Just because an activity is lawful or natural does not make it beneficial. He will not be mastered by his impulses, especially impulses that prove unhelpful.

What kind of impulse is unhelpful? For Paul, it is one that seeks its reward in temporary gratification. Take, for instance, the impulse of hunger. Nothing is more natural than eating. According to an old aphorism, "Food is meant for the stomach and the stomach for food" (1 Cor. 6:13). The two were made for each other. But just because the stomach yearns for food does not mean a person should eat without restraint, especially for temporary gratification. And eating is a temporal activity. Neither food nor the stomach is made to endure: "God will destroy both one and the other" (1 Cor. 6:13). Hence consumption of food ought to be moderated. We must not allow the body to be governed by an impulse whose benefits are only temporary. That is unhelpful. Instead, we should focus on more enduring pursuits.

Pressing the point further, Paul turns to a second impulse—the appetite for sexual gratification. Here he creates his own maxim: "The body is not meant for sexual immorality" (v. 13). These are provocative words because they imply that not all sex is good sex. Sometimes sex is immoral. This is a judgment patently at odds with the licentious spirit of the first century, where people engaged in almost any kind of sexual activity as long as it was felt not to be injurious to others. But here Paul censures a whole spectrum of sexual behavior. He uses the word *porneia*, from which we derive the English term "pornography." It refers to any kind of sexual activity outside the union of marriage. Paul is opposing extramarital sex.

To the Corinthians this would sound like an outlandish prohibition. Who was Paul to issue such a radical edict? How could he be so prudish and antisocial? Yet in the apostle's mind, he is only promulgating common sense. Like food, sex represents temporary gratification. Like immoderate eating, unregulated sex is injurious to the human body. Those who endorse sexual freedom must reckon with its disheartening consequences. *Porneia* can slice into its participants like the unsanitary thrust of a rusty blade. It can leave festering wounds. It can drain vitality from human souls. It can imprison people in stifling addictions. Clearly, it can be anything but helpful. The body is not meant for sexual immorality.

The Delight of Cruciform Sex

What, then, is the body meant for? According to Paul, "The body is . . . for the Lord, and the Lord for the body" (1 Cor. 6:13). In other words it is designed for the Lord's service ("the body is . . . for the Lord") and equipped for that service by the Lord himself ("the Lord is for the body"). The human body could scarcely possess a more lofty purpose. It is an exalted instrument in the hands of almighty God. What could bring greater personal delight than to glorify the Lord with our bodies?

And as time stretches into eternity, the delight only increases. One day the God who raised the Lord Jesus will also raise us up by his power (1 Cor. 6:14), and when that day arrives, our bodies will be liberated from the corrosive effects of sin and bring even greater glory to God. The assurance that our delight will multiply as time gives way to eternity ought to add to our present comfort. What could be more comforting than to know that, beginning now and lasting forever, we can use our bodies to bring increasing increments of glory to the Lord?

Here is a satisfaction which transcends any temporal gratification. Unlike the yearning for food or for sex, which always leaves us hankering for more, we find full satisfaction in the assurance that our bodies will be eternally useful to God. Nothing could so invigorate the soul. Nothing could so animate our daily existence. Indeed, the assurance provides eternal refreshment at the deepest level of our beings. As Malcolm Muggeridge puts it: "What, I ask myself, does life hold, what is there in the works of time, in the past, now, and to come, which could possibly be put in the balance against the refreshment of . . . the living water that Christ alone offers to the spiritually thirsty?"[2] The answer is absolutely nothing! Nothing could bring more refreshment than knowing that our bodies will forever be useful in the service of Christ. Such a prospect is water to parched souls.

Too seldom, however, do we drink from this well. Delight in the Lord is easily neglected. We are distracted by temporary pleasures. How do we stay focused on refreshment that is spiritual? Paul continues his instruction by posing a rhetorical question: "Do you not know that your bodies are members of Christ?" (1 Cor. 6:15). The implication is staggering: our bodies are actually extensions of Jesus Christ. We serve in our world as mini-embodiments of the Lord himself. To see us in our bodily existence is to see a member of Jesus.

What featured most prominently in the earthly life of Christ ought therefore to feature most prominently in ours. Since the most compelling feature of the Lord's existence was, as we have seen, his willingness to lay down his life for the good of others, the same sort of sacrificial service ought to be evident in our bodily existence. And when it is, when we use our bodies to serve others, we discover that we are deeply fulfilled as human beings. Replicating the cruciform love of Jesus Christ maximizes our personal delight. This in turn sheds new and helpful light on the vexing subject of sex.

CONTRARY IMPULSES

Paul returns to the matter of human sexuality by asking another rhetorical question: "Shall I then take the members of Christ and make them members of a prostitute?" (1 Cor. 6:15). The question is meant to elicit an emphatic—never! Nothing could be more contrary to the purposes of God than for a Christian to unite with a prostitute. The reason is embedded in yet another rhetorical question. "Do you not know that he who is joined to a prostitute becomes one body with her? For, as it is written, 'The two will become one flesh'" (1 Cor. 6:16). To become one with a prostitute while also being one with Christ is a logical impossibility. The two unions are mutually exclusive. That is because they are governed by countervailing impulses. The person who is united to Christ is motivated by self-emptying love, while the person who joins himself to a prostitute succumbs to self-grasping lust.

The two impulses are not just different from each other, they are diametrical opposites. They cannot coexist in the same body. Underscoring the incompatibility, Paul reminds his readers that those who have been "joined to the Lord [become] one spirit with him" (1 Cor. 6:17). They are moved by the very spirit that moved the Lord, which we know to be the spirit of self-giving love.

Thus Paul has no option but to issue the following exhortation: "Flee from sexual immorality" (1 Cor. 6:18). He supports the admonition with bracing logic: "Every other sin a person commits is outside the body, but the sexually immoral person sins against his own body" (1 Cor. 6:18). Extramarital sex, Paul insists, is damaging to the human body. It is therefore a sin against the body—the sin of using the body in a way contrary to its created purpose. The body was made to give glory to God through acts of sacrificial service. When it is used to pursue the fleeting pleasure of sexual immorality, it exchanges its role as the bearer of God's image for a very dark counterfeit. No longer a beacon of self-emptying love, it succumbs to degenerating lusts. The misuse of our bodies not only betrays our position as creatures made in God's image, it also drains our bodies of vitality. It is a sin against our own bodies.

TAKING A STAND

This is a frightful critique. It is also the sort of critique that would have reduced Paul to a laughingstock among his peers. But he does not flinch. His resolve is firm. No doubt it is because of his travels from marketplace to marketplace in the leading cities of the Greco-Roman world, where he has witnessed not only an onslaught of sexual images and licentious behavior but also the devastating carnage—in terms of withered souls and damaged lives—of people who worship at the altar of Aphrodite. He has noted well the fading light in the eyes of his immoral contemporaries. He has anguished deeply over the sexual decay within the realm of Caesar. What person with even a modicum of human compassion could in circumstances like these not issue an urgent warning: flee sexual immorality! It might not be well received, but how else could a loving apostle alert his beleaguered fellow human beings to the danger of their spiritual and physical demise?

We need such a warning today. In a world intoxicated by sex, we need to hear afresh the words of the apostle Paul. We need to flee sexual immorality. We need to protect our souls from an avalanche of sensual images. We need to unplug the Internet (or install an effective filter) when its contents imprison us in dark worlds of sexual fantasy. We need to reassess relationships quickly when lust becomes a burning obsession. We need to cease frequenting places where couples pair off and indulge in sexual desires. We need to be aggressive and uncompromising in our resolve to flee sexual immorality. The vitality of our bodies depends on it. We need to stand up and courageously protect what is so valuable—the use of our bodies for the glory of the Lord—from what is so destructive—sex outside of marriage.

GLORIFYING GOD WITH OUR BODIES

In addition to all we have learned from the apostle Paul, there is an even greater inducement to sexual purity. Up to this point, Paul has provided only negative incentives. He has told us what not to do and why not to do it. Flee sexual immorality . . . it is a sin against the body. There is great value in such prohibitions; it is always helpful to know what to *flee from* and why. Yet it is more helpful to know what to *run toward* and why. Without positive motivation, most of us fail at our objectives. This is especially true in the arena of sex. We are much more likely to rise to Paul's exalted sexual ethic if we are propelled by a lofty vision.

Paul now presents that vision. "Do you not know that your body is a temple of the Holy Spirit within you, whom you have from God? You are not your own, for you were bought with a price. So glorify God in your body" (1 Cor. 6:19–20). According to these words, the human body is meant to be the habitation of the most exalted personage in the universe. Purchased at the price of the shed blood of his Son, our bodies are to be God's home.

It is impossible to comprehend this truth fully, but one dramatic implication stands out: if our bodies are the abode of God, then they ought to reflect his indwelling presence, and especially his matchless love. As people who house the glory of God, we have the privilege of replicating the cruciform love of Jesus Christ. With a calling as exalted as this, how could we trifle with self-seeking pleasures? How could we entertain behavior that would empty our lives of this glory?

To the person who struggles with the powerful enticements of sex—and who of us does not?—from the temptation of pornography to the allure of adultery, here is the surest path to victory and the greatest incentive to sexual purity: *a passion to use your body for the glory of Christ.* To cherish his glory more than anything else, above everything else, before anything else, instead of everything else—this alone provides sufficient motivation for the elevation of our behavior above destructive lusts. And when we passionately seek the Lord's glory, a miracle happens: we undergo a metamorphosis. We are "transformed into the same image from one degree of glory to another" (2 Cor. 3:18). The glory of the Lord rubs off on us, indeed rubs off *in* us!

This is a truth that has surfaced over and over again in our study of marriage: we bring glory to God by reproducing an image of his glory in our daily lives, *by replicating the self-giving love of the cross of Christ.* And it is precisely this truth that leads us to a vibrant and satisfying sexuality within marriage.

We are now in position to apply Paul's teaching in 1 Corinthians to the sexual union of husbands and wives. Nothing invigorates the act of sexual intercourse like an embodiment, in both partners, of the Spirit of Christ. Nothing encourages sexual intimacy like an exhibition, in both partners, of the self-giving image of God. Nothing insures sexual fulfillment like a commitment, on the part of both partners, to make the pleasure of the other their principal aim and focus.

Sex is not intended to be a frenzied pursuit of temporal gratification, as it so often is portrayed in our narcissistic age; rather, it flourishes best and is most satisfying when husbands and wives seek to serve the needs of the other. When the self-giving love of Christ is replicated in the physical interaction of two believers, it catapults the sexual experience to peaks of fulfillment.

EXCLUSIVE PLEASURES

The delight of God-glorifying sex is depicted unabashedly in the biblical book of Proverbs. There we encounter a father who implores his son to take care how he indulges his sexual desires. "Drink water from your own cistern, flowing water from your own well" (Prov. 5:15). In other words, make sure you draw refreshment from the person who belongs to you. Do not imbibe pleasures indiscriminately. "Should your springs be scattered abroad, streams of water in the streets?" (Prov. 5:16). May it never be! Sexual love—the subject of this chapter of Proverbs—is too precious for careless dispersal. Until you find the woman into whom you will pour all your affections, keep the waters of love sacred. "Let them be for yourself alone, and not for strangers with you" (Prov. 5:17).

It takes discipline to restrain sexual impulses, but it is well worth the effort. The father points forward to a day when the son will receive his reward in full, when sexual love will climax in the profoundest joy. "Let your fountain be blessed, and rejoice in the wife of your youth, a lovely deer, a graceful doe" (Prov. 5:18–19). It will be a moment of unparalleled satisfaction, and not just because of the love that flows out to this doe but also because of the love that flows in. "Let her breasts fill you at all times with delight; be intoxicated always in her love" (Prov. 5:19).

The great discovery of sexual love is that when it flows according to God's design, the output is almost always surpassed by the intake. When both partners spare no effort to make the physical union fulfilling to the other, both receive an explosive measure of delight in return. The glory of sex is maximized when husbands and wives seek sacrificially to empty themselves into the other, when they resolve mutually to pursue the highest pleasure of the other. When two people give themselves up in this way, sexual intimacy becomes thrilling beyond words. And it certainly lends credence to the final piece of wisdom offered by the father in this passage: "Why should you be intoxicated, my son, with a forbidden woman and embrace the bosom of an adulteress?" (Prov. 5:20).

So true. Sexual love thrives best in a closed union. It produces optimum delight when it is reserved for the marriage partner alone. It is maximally enjoyed when it is exclusively given.

That is also the message of the smitten romantics in the Song of Solomon. Their sensual attraction to each other—and it could scarcely be more erotic—is animated by the shared conviction that they belong to each other alone. "My beloved is mine, and I am his" (Song 2:16; 6:3). The young woman views the sexual love of her partner as her exclusive domain and insists that he remain devoted to her alone. "Set me as a seal upon your heart" (Song 8:6). Sexual love is too precious for interlopers. Rivals must be rebuffed and "jealousy is fierce as the grave" (Song 8:6). Each partner must be vigilant in the preservation of marital purity and tenaciously throw off any temptation which might compromise the bond. This is priceless wisdom. Husbands and wives, may nothing violate our sexual unions (Heb. 13:4)!

VERBAL INTERCOURSE

Perhaps the best way to create vibrant sexual intimacy is to excel at verbal communication. This is a common theme in the Song of Solomon. For a poem designed as a tribute to erotic love, we are amazed how little we see of the movements beneath the sheets and how much we are allowed to eavesdrop on the verbal interaction of the two lovers. The husband and the wife seem to know that successful lovemaking is 10 percent perspiration and 90 percent conversation! Listen to the man as he heaps praise on his beloved:

> Behold, you are beautiful, my love,
>> behold, you are beautiful!
>> Your eyes are doves. . .
> Your hair is like a flock of goats
>> leaping down the slopes of Gilead.
> Your teeth are like a flock of shorn ewes
>> that have come up from the washing, . . .
> Your lips are like a scarlet thread,
>> and your mouth is lovely.
> Your cheeks are like halves of a pomegranate. . .
> Your neck is like the tower of David,
>> built in rows of stone, . . .
> Your two breasts are like two fawns, . . .

You are altogether beautiful, my love;
there is no flaw in you. . . .
You have captivated my heart, my sister, my bride;
you have captivated my heart with one glance of your
eyes, . . .
How beautiful is your love, my sister, my bride!
How much better is your love than wine,
and the fragrance of your oils than any spice!
Your lips drip nectar, my bride;
honey and milk are under your tongue. (Song 4:1–11)

While the words may sound archaic to us, they nevertheless reveal how well the man knows his woman. He has observed her at close range and is able to compose colorful metaphors in celebration of her charms. Clearly he has put time and work into the verbal tribute. Long before the lights dim and passions heat up, he gives himself to her in words. And she returns the blessing:

My beloved is radiant and ruddy,
distinguished among ten thousand.
His head is the finest gold;
his locks are wavy,
black as a raven.
His eyes are like doves
beside streams of water,
bathed in milk,
sitting beside a full pool.
His cheeks are like beds of spices,
mounds of sweet-smelling herbs.
His lips are lilies,
dripping liquid myrrh.
His arms are rods of gold,
set with jewels.
His body is polished ivory,
bedecked with sapphires.
His legs are alabaster columns,
set on bases of gold.

His appearance is like Lebanon,
   choice as the cedars.
His mouth is most sweet,
   and he is altogether desirable.
This is my beloved and this is my friend. (Song 5:10–16)

The true beauty of these verbal tapestries is that there are indeed two verbal tapestries. Each partner pours into the other the encouragement of a well-crafted tribute.

And notice the distinguishing feature of each composition—it is marked by *positive* affirmations. From the mouths of this amorous couple comes only effusive praise. We find no hint of criticism or correction or even unsolicited advice. It is just unrestrained adoration. Is this kind of consistently positive support really possible in marriage? If it is not, then the basis for mutually fulfilling sex is seriously imperiled.

How important it is to work at elevating our marital conversations, dispensing with the verbal jabs and specializing instead in uplifting encouragement. It is essential to build each other up, and not just in anticipation of an exciting sexual encounter. The entire marriage should be marked by creative expressions of mutual admiration. "Gracious words are like a honeycomb, sweetness to the soul and health to the body," and "A word fitly spoken is like apples of gold in a setting of silver" (Prov. 16:24; 25:11).

Every competent marital counselor will work to improve lines of communication between husbands and wives. Poor verbal interaction lies at the root of almost every marital rift. Too often, however, marital advice consists of techniques designed to improve interaction in times of conflict and disagreement. The approach of the Song of Solomon is different. In the case of our two romantics, good communication is encouraged not just when difficulties arise and sexual love is impaired, but at all times. When the entire marital union is marked by positive affirmations from both partners, an atmosphere is created in which sexual intercourse can thrive. And the two romantics in the Song of Solomon provide the correct pattern. It is only *after* each

117

inundates the other with verbal praise that "my beloved come[s] to his garden, and eat[s] its choicest fruits" (Song 4:16).

THE SECRET GARDEN

What actually happens in that garden? What is the nature of the fruits that the two consume? Answers to these questions are elusive, even in an explicit love poem like the Song of Solomon. The account of what transpires when the dashing young husband leads his beautiful wife into the chamber of love is conspicuously short on details, except for the tantalizing revelation that "his left hand is under my head, and his right hand embraces me" (Song 2:6; 8:3), a position of hands and head possible only when two are lying down together. In a day when sexual secrets are trotted out salaciously for public consumption, we naturally want to know more about the erotic love-making of this handsome couple.

But do we really? Is it not enough to know that they have passed behind the curtain of love and will shortly fill each other with stores of affection held in reserve for the ecstasy of just this moment, that they will create for each other a garden of pleasure whose fruits will be uniquely their own, that they will luxuriate in a connection so intimate and so exciting that to publish its details would be to turn something sacred into something common? It is enough for the witnesses of that day, the so-called "choristers," simply to pay tribute to the words of affection expressed between the man and the woman and leave the rest, the holy consummation, to the couple itself. It is the *imagined* joy of the two lovers that prompts a song of discreet celebration: "We will exult and rejoice in you; we will extol your love more than wine" (Song 1:4). Sexual love, pure and undefiled, is better than the finest of wines, indeed better than just about anything else.

For many years, the Song of Solomon was viewed as a symbolic portrait of the love of Christ. In particular, the selfless love of the two lovers was felt to bear a striking resemblance to Christ's love for the church. But the Song of Solomon must be viewed first within its original context, a context which, as we have seen, provides insight into the consummating act of marriage. And the lesson is clear: two bodies fuse most perfectly and most blissfully when the words and caresses of each partner are marked by self-giving love.

But by providing a breathtaking picture of the joys of sexual love, the Song of Solomon also anticipates the Love which would find its ultimate expression on the splintered beams of a Roman cross. Even in sex, especially in sex, we see an image of the crucified Lord. In the selfless physical interaction of two lovers we see an anticipation—at least in part—of the cruciform love of Jesus. In fact, sexual love reaches its zenith when husbands and wives reproduce in their union an image of the sacrificial love of the Savior.

The same friend whose words were cited in the opening paragraphs of this chapter, the friend who stood up and provided a stirring tribute to his parents-in-law on the occasion of their fiftieth anniversary, also volunteered, as this chapter was being composed, the following piece of counsel. "I trust you will reinforce the benefits of consistent and mutually fulfilling physical intimacy within marriage. It takes work. It requires effective communication. But the relational dividends are myriad."

That is precisely God's message to us, a message as breathtaking and relevant today as it ever has been. Husbands and wives, you can be fused in body to the glory of God. Go, create, and celebrate!

IN GOD'S CHURCH

What a blessed thing is the marriage of two believers, of one hope, one discipline, servants of the same Master! Together they offer up their prayers—together they lie in the dust, teaching each other, exhorting each other, bearing up each other. They are together in God's Church, together at God's feast, together in straits, persecutions, consolations.

TERTULLIAN

Trekking through the mangled forest was excruciating. It was old-growth timber deep in the Canadian north, and the deadfall, along with an underlying layer of decomposing plant matter, presented obstacles that made the going almost impossible. In one step a boot could easily sink, as through a trapdoor, into a web of tangled decay, becoming wedged so tightly amid submerged logs that agonizing minutes would be required for its extraction.

Meanwhile, clouds of mosquitoes assaulted exposed faces, and thorns from blackberry bushes ripped through clothing and tore at the skin. There was nothing redeeming about the landscape. Dark and dank, stifling and impenetrable—the climbing party felt like the imprisoned souls in Samuel Beckett's cylinder, desperate for any kind of escape. But there was no escape. After days of futile bushwhacking, hope gave way to despair. The men of the mountains were lost, hopelessly lost.

Suddenly a call was raised by a scout at the head of the party. He had rounded a corner and surmounted a huge pile of boulders and was arrested by a sight so dazzling that even his exuberant cry failed to prepare the others for what they were about to witness. Stretching out in front of them for mile after mile was a lake too beautiful for words. Doubtless the misery of the expedition served to magnify the joy of discovery—a foot in hell usually makes a foot elsewhere seem like heaven. But even today, more than a hundred years after the original discovery, the sight of Medicine Lake leaves unsuspecting tourists, who round the same corner and circumnavigate the same pile of boulders, absolutely spellbound.

MANY TRIBUTARIES, ONE BODY OF WATER

What is the secret of this lake? In a word, its ethereal color—an iridescent azure so surreal that it seems to come straight from the palette of Peter Paul Rubens, the Renaissance painter whose mastery of colors mesmerized the cognoscenti of his day. But no human brush stroke could ever duplicate the sublimity of this body of water. True to its name, the lake works its medicine on its surroundings—trees which would otherwise cast only sinister shadows across a dreary landscape now dance in tribute to the glorious lake, encircling it brightly with an evergreen frame. It is a testament to what a lake can do to its environment.

How does Medicine Lake achieve its magical color? Scientists have discovered that its water emanates from a surprising variety of sources. Some comes from snowmelt, rushing down from high altitudes, cascading over faces of sheer granite, and carrying microscopic traces of high-country sediment in its molecules. Some comes from underground caverns, chambers full of exotic minerals, the residue of which is borne away by streams into the awaiting lake. Perhaps most fascinating of all is that some comes from highways of ice called glaciers, whose crushing weight pulverizes the bedrock below and churns up particles infinitesimally small which also make their way into the lake. It is this amalgamation of tributaries, carrying a wide variety of sediment from vastly different sources, that gives Medicine Lake its extraordinary color. When the rays of the sun alight on the billions of particles suspended in the water, a reaction occurs that produces a shade of blue so unearthly that even Rubens would blush in amazement. It is the conjunction of these molecules that refashions an otherwise gloomy landscape into a masterpiece of exquisite color.

Medicine Lake is a gift of God to the natural world, but it is by no means his greatest gift. That distinction belongs not to a body of water but to a body of people—a collection of diverse human beings from a large assortment of backgrounds whose union in one body provides a more vibrant reflection of God's glory than any other spectacle in creation.

MANY MEMBERS, ONE BODY OF CHRIST

These are the people of the body of Christ. They are drawn together not by gravity but by the irresistible call of God himself. "God arranged the members in the body, each one of them, as he chose" (1 Cor. 12:18). And each person arrives, not with sediment derived from the journey but with a gift from God, a supernatural bequest, a specific and unique ability. It is a gift designed to be given away— given to other members of the body for the growth of the body. It thus bears a striking resemblance to the greatest gift of all: Jesus Christ. He gave himself away as a ransom for many (Mark 10:45).

It is hardly surprising that people called by God to give their gifts away are known as the body *of Christ*. They conform to Christ in every way. They receive gifts "according to the measure of Christ's gift" (Eph. 4:7). They give away their gifts "to equip the saints" (Eph. 4:12), and as a result, the whole body grows "up in every way into him" (Eph. 4:15). And when every member is pouring his or her gifts into the others, the body attains a unity which reflects "the measure of the stature of the fullness of Christ" (Eph. 4:13). Looking at this body of people, you see Christ himself.

Where is this extraordinary body to be found? That we must ask betrays our unfamiliarity with one of the cardinal doctrines of the Bible—the doctrine of the local church. Many years ago when driving the English churchman John Stott from the train station to the place where he was scheduled to preach, I asked him to identify the doctrine he considered most neglected among contemporary Christians. Without hesitation, he responded "Ecclesiology!"—by which he meant the doctrine of the local church.

It was the answer I least expected. But over the years, I have come to see the wisdom of his reply. How many fail to acknowledge the fundamental importance of this unique body? It is the epicenter of God's work in the world. It bears the name of his Son: the body of Christ. It is where the work of the Lord reaches its fullest expression. It is the organ by which God is reclaiming all things for his glory (Eph. 1:22–23). The local church—there is no more strategic body in the entire world.

LOVE AND THE LOCAL CHURCH

The fruit of the church can be summed up by one word: love. The exhortation of Paul to local churches never varies: "Put on love, which binds everything together in perfect harmony" (Col. 3:14); "Owe no one anything, except to love each other, for the one who loves another has fulfilled the law" (Rom. 13:8); "So now faith, hope, and love abide, these three; but the greatest of these is love" (1 Cor. 13:13); "Through love serve one another. For the whole law is fulfilled in one word: 'You shall love your neighbor as yourself'" (Gal. 5:13–14); "May the Lord make you increase and abound in love for one another" (1 Thess. 3:12).

A similar call is issued by the apostle John: "This is the message that you have heard from the beginning, that we should love one another" (1 John 3:11); "Beloved, let us love one another, for love is from God" (1 John 4:7). So also the apostle Peter: "Above all, keep loving one another" (1 Pet. 4:8). The exhortations of the apostles of course reflect the words of Jesus himself: "By this all people will know that you are my disciples, if you have love for one another" (John 13:35).

But the apostles are doing more than reflecting the *words* of Jesus; they are also drawing inspiration from the central *deed* of his ministry: his cross. There we see the most radical expression of love in history, total self-sacrifice—"by this we know love, that he laid down his life for us, and we ought to lay down our lives for the brothers" (1 John 3:16).

Members of the body of Christ, those called by God into the local church, must take note. It is our vocation to embody together the cruciform love of Jesus Christ. To us the call has been raised:

"Walk in love, as Christ loved us [when he] gave himself up for us" (Eph. 5:2).

Examples of how this love works out in practice are ubiquitous in apostolic letters to local churches: "Bear one another's burdens, and so fulfill the law of Christ" (Gal. 6:2); "Look . . . to the interests of others. Have this mind among yourselves, which is yours in Christ Jesus" (Phil. 2:4–5); "Always seek to do good to one another" (1 Thess. 5:15); "Be kind to one another, tenderhearted, forgiving one another" (Eph. 4:32); "Rejoice with those who rejoice, weep with those who weep. Live in harmony with one another" (Rom. 12:15–16). Additional examples could be multiplied almost indefinitely, for there is no limit to the ways in which a local church can manifest something as boundless as Christ's love.

Here is a point worth noting. This love represents a radical foil to the world in which we live. Our society is riddled by lovelessness. While the word *love* still features prominently in social discourse, true love, biblical love, rarely surfaces in the world of the "selfish gene."

And its absence is disheartening. How many people today try to put one foot in front of the other and sustain a meaningful existence but sink constantly into a tangled web of frustration? Looking for friendship, they receive only wounds of the soul. Craving companionship, they become mired in loneliness. Seeking acceptance, they fall into self-pity. Yearning for security, they are wracked by anxiety. Weary people, just like those of the lost expedition of old, are marooned in a dark and mangled forest, with so little satisfaction, and yet they forge ahead looking for solace in anything that might distract them from their empty lives—a screen, a beer, a dalliance. When these, too, fail, desperation sets in and they begin to wish—begin to pray—that a cry might be raised by someone farther up the trail who can draw their attention to something beautiful and banish their despair forever.

What possibly could bring such relief? There is a striking answer: it is the sight of something so radiant that it actually transforms its surroundings. It is the sight of the body of Christ. It is a glimpse of the local church—the local church in action, members interacting lovingly with fellow members, pouring out God-given gifts into one another, showcasing in that gift-giving, in that relentless service, the dazzling glory of the sacrificial love of Jesus Christ.

It is precisely this love that is so absent in society—the love without which human souls wither and die, the love for which humans (whether they know it or not) passionately crave. And it is found preeminently in the local church. The body of Christ is the antidote to a loveless world.

MARRIAGE AND THE LOCAL CHURCH

What does all this have to do with marriage? Much in every way. The remarkable organism called the local church is, at its root, a kaleidoscope of couples. Those who are "God's choosen ones, holy and beloved" are grouped by Paul in terms of pairs—husbands and wives, parents and children, employers and employees (Eph. 5:22–6:9; Col. 3:12, 18–4:1). Each of these relational units represents one of the three fundamental building blocks of society. Every person in the world, including every single person, is either a product of or a participant in a marriage (husbands and wives), a family (parents and children), and/or a business (employers and employees).

But the significance of these relational pairs derives not from their presence in every society but from their presence in the very first society, in the society initially assembled by God. From the earliest chapters of the Bible, the human race was constituted in terms of interpersonal units and in terms of these three units in particular.

The same pattern has always marked God's people, and it marks the body of Christ today. The local church is meant to serve as a model for society and not *vice versa*. In its interpersonal relations, and especially in the ecclesial relations of marriages, families, and businesses, the local church provides the paradigms for similar relationships in the world outside.

This leads to a dramatic conclusion. In the economy of God, the local church is designed to be a home base for the marriages of God's people. It is the organism not just where weddings are performed but where couples put down roots and establish a base of operations. It is the marital home. It is where husbands and wives derive their meaning and mission in life and from which they minister to the world around them. Or to put it another way, the church family is the body through which nuclear families (husbands and wives) manifest the glory of the triune family (Father, Son, and Holy Spirit) to a world of families.

How many husbands and wives view the local church as their primary base of operations? The number is probably very small. We give priority to other things, the things that occupy our time—earning an income, maintaining a residence, raising a family—and the venues of these things become our bases of operation: the office, the home, and the school. We look at the local church as just one of the many cogs in our marriages, not the axle on which our marriages rotate. This is unfortunate, because something enormously important is being forfeited, both for marriage and for the world outside. To view the local church as ancillary to marriage—a welcome distraction from the affairs of life but not the center of life itself—is to miss out on one of the most explosive and far-reaching blessings of the marital union.

LOVE MULTIPLYING EXPONENTIALLY

Here we must peer deeply into the dynamics of a local church. Love, as we have seen, is the principal vocation of the local church, and love, as we have also seen, possesses a miraculous capacity to bind people together. In the case of husbands and wives who love each other with the love of Christ, love binds them into one flesh. But— prepare yourselves for an exciting truth—the love which husbands and wives share together does not find its end point in their union. When two people love each other with Christ's love, something dynamic happens: they not only fuse into one but also discover that their love begins to multiply exponentially. The love they now possess together is bigger than the love they first emptied into each other. The love of Christ, when passed back and forth between husbands and wives, creates a surplus of love.

But love, the most valuable commodity in the world, must not be wasted. What happens when couples are filled with more love than they can spend on each other? According to the plan of God, they pour it into members of the local church. Indeed, that is one reason why husbands and wives make the body of Christ their base of operations. *The love multiplying between them is meant to spill over onto others in the church family.* And when the surplus love of marriages is in turn passed back and forth among other members of the body, additional multiplications occur and the volume of love increases even more, which causes still further love to spill out into the lives of other members of the body in an almost endless multiplication of love. The local church is overflowing with love!

The phenomenon may be compared to nuclear fission. Atoms are among the tiniest and most unnoticed wonders of nature, and yet they wield almost supernatural strength. When an atom is split and united with other split atoms, a cataclysmic reaction is created: an explosion of nuclear energy capable of turning on the lights of entire cities. How can such tiny and seemingly insignificant atoms produce such a colossal display of power? In my younger days, I would ponder this very question while surfing offshore from the nuclear power plant at San Onofre, California. While waiting for a good wave, I would gaze at the immense dome and marvel at the thousands of utility pylons arranged like a well-ordered army to convey massive quantities of energy from particles so small they are invisible to the naked eye. It was a mind-boggling sight.

Yet the energy of nuclear fission is insignificant compared to the power welling up within a local church. When the love of husbands and wives mingles with the love of other members of the body of Christ, a dramatic series of "explosions" takes place, reaction upon reaction, with enough energy not just to electrify cities of neon lights and microwave ovens but, far more importantly, to bring spiritual light to a world dying in darkness.

Like Medicine Lake to the eyes of bedraggled mountain men, like nuclear fission to households without electricity, the glory of the local church can literally electrify this world. And what is the primal unit of the local church, the first of the couples listed by the apostle

Paul? Two tiny atoms—a wife and a husband—united by expressions of cruciform love, produce within their marriage a reaction of surplus love, which in turn spills out onto other members of the local church, among whom additional reactions take place. This generates within the church family such a surfeit of love that the surrounding world, suffering from a chronic absence of just that love, lifts up its collective eyes and celebrates the Source of this love and glorifies the Father in heaven (Matt. 5:16).

HUSBANDS AND WIVES IN THE LOCAL CHURCH

For too long we have viewed the local church as an addendum to marriage, as a place where people gather for worship, where they are stirred (hopefully) by powerful preaching and engaging music, where they enjoy weekly reunions with friends, where they recite their wedding vows, and where, at last, they will lie motionlessly as friends gather in their memory. It is the place where we receive encouragement. While that image of the local church is certainly valid and even to be applauded, we have discovered now a more important reality of the local church. It is the place where we give encouragement.

This is such an important insight that it is tempting to encourage husbands and wives to abandon all prior assumptions about the local church and to draw a bead on this one amazing truth. Too often we are told that healthy marriages depend on loving communities and too seldom that healthy communities depend on loving marriages. Too often we stress the importance of shepherding marriages within the context of local churches, providing godly marital counsel, consistent accountability, and loving oversight, and yet (while not in any way wanting to diminish the value of shepherding) there is an even more strategic biblical emphasis for marriage. It is the teaching that husbands and wives ought to invest themselves in the ministry of the local church, spreading their surplus love among members of the body of Christ.

Young couples just setting out on the adventure of marriage should make it a priority to find a local church where they can serve together. Husbands and wives who have been married for years should likewise, if they have not done so already, look for a local family of believers into whom they can pour their love.

When ten days of honeymoon in Paris came to an end, Charles and Susannah Spurgeon returned eagerly to London. "What a pure and unsullied joy was that home-coming!"[1] wrote Susannah later. How could a homecoming possibly surpass the nuptial bliss of Paris? For the Spurgeons, it was returning to serve together in the work of God through the local church. It topped everything else.

Surpassing joy—I have witnessed it firsthand in the faces of many brothers and sisters in Christ: husbands and wives who open their home every week to large groups of students, teaching them about Christ and cooking them a meal; other couples who adopt grown children challenged by learning disabilities or by social ostracism; still others who mortgage their home in order to pay for the landscaping that enables the church to obtain an occupancy permit; others who prepare and deliver meals regularly to new mothers or the ailing; others who on weeknights squeeze into a small booth to run the sound system for leadership training sessions; others who forfeit a summer vacation to serve on a church mission to children of Rwanda orphaned by genocide; others who manage the church nursery, caring for the next generation, stocking and supplying, decorating and cleaning; and others who lead choirs of children who sing in church to the glory of God.

Examples like these could be multiplied endlessly, but it would make for a very long book! The point is this: incomparable joy reverberates in the hearts of husbands and wives who unite together in ministry within the local church of Jesus Christ. In the words of Tertullian, "What a blessing is the marriage of two believers . . . they are together in God's church!"

Does this mean that couples should avoid serving outside the local church? No. Closest to my heart is the example of a husband and a wife who invested themselves in multiple ministries for the Lord. The husband was a land developer in Southern California and his wife was a devoted mother of two young children. He sat on the boards of several parachurch organizations, and she maintained regular contact with missionaries round the globe. But there was never any doubt in their minds that the local church was their primary base of operations. When on Saturday evenings they opened the doors of their home to the youth of the community for the study of God's Word, for prayer, for fellowship, and for food, their eyes sparkled with a radiant joy. Long past my bedtime, I would sneak over to the corner of the fireplace to catch a glimpse of that radiance. I learned early what filled the hearts of my mom and my dad. It was the work of Christ through the local church.

If you are married, do not rest until you obtain the ultimate marital blessing; look for a good, Christ-centered local church. Then ring up the pastor, talk to the elders, corral the deacons, accost a parishioner—ask them where in the body of Christ you might begin to serve. Become committed participants in the world's most strategic organism.

A FOIL TO POSTMARITAL SOCIETY

We live in a day of unprecedented relational confusion, and many of the perplexities center on the institution of marriage. Unlike other periods of history, people today discuss marriage and homosexuality as though the two existed on equal terms; people jettison the priority of marriage for the convenience of cohabitation (soon to number half of all male and female unions), and they terminate existing marriages in staggering numbers (with almost half of all unions ending in divorce). The confusion is taking a toll on society in general, and especially on its children, nearly half of whom will grow up in homes without the presence of one natural parent. In other words, a majority of tomorrow's world is being denied what has long been regarded as a fundamental entitlement, the proximate and loving nurture of both parents, and hence will grow up confused about the most basic of all human relationships—marriage. How can we stem the confusion?

God has always ministered to a troubled world through a collection of people. He has always provided one family amid a sea of dysfunctional families to minister the glory of his love. Today that one family is the local church. It is why biblical authors implore us to "consider how to stir up one another to love and good works, not neglecting to meet together" (Heb. 10:24–25). It is through the love and good works of local churches that the world receives an alternative to interrelational discord. The local church is a family in the world for the world, a family of families reflecting to the world's families the glory of the triune family of God. For the love-deprived children of earth, there could hardly be a more beautiful illustration of family than the local church of Jesus Christ.

Many local churches seek to address relational confusion by supporting political (profamily legislation) or religious (national days of prayer) initiatives. These approaches certainly have merit. They highlight legitimate social ills and forestall greater decay. But they can never foster the sort of internal change, the sort of heart change, necessary to produce truly healthy societies. For this reason, they must not be allowed to drain resources and time from the ultimate mission of the local church: to proclaim the glory of God in the cross of Jesus Christ.

It has always been easier to sponsor legislation and to attend prayer meetings than to seek the miracle of God-glorifying marriages. How many local churches are prepared to do the hard work of building strong marriages? How many are ready to reach out to troubled husbands and wives in the community and introduce them to the ways of Christ? How many are willing to pray that the Lord would confer his righteousness to couples dying in their sins and then fill them with his love? How many local churches are eager to minister to this world? How many are able to minister to this world? The answer to the last question is very encouraging: far more than we begin to realize.

The resources of God for local churches, and for husbands and wives committed to local churches, are inexhaustible. Once again the mysterious lake in Canada provides an apt illustration. Every year when seepage depletes Medicine Lake, people begin to wonder whether the water will vanish altogether. So far it has never happened. No matter how much of its volume drains into subterranean caves, Medicine Lake always remains viable.

We now know why: it is replenished each year by a much larger body of water higher up the canyon. Because of the "malignancies" endured in the discovery of this higher reservoir—injuries, exhaustion, hunger—it was given the name Maligne Lake by the exasperated explorer who took one look at the lake, turned around, and headed back down the valley. Both the name and the hasty retreat were unfortunate. In the minds of many world travelers, Maligne Lake ranks as one of the world's most breathtaking bodies of water. It is also the second largest glacier-fed lake in North America and thus serves as an inexhaustible resource for its smaller sister below.

The local church is also the beneficiary of a greater resource. No less than a full complement of the love of God is available to the body of Christ. Its members never need to wonder whether their resources will be sufficient to refresh the dysfunctional world around them. There is only one question: will their willingness be sufficient? Knowing that their resources are illimitable will fortify their willingness.

A MAGNIFICENT PORTRAIT

The members arrive from many places and possess many gifts, drawn together by the invisible hand of God. Their group portrait is stunning. Whenever the rays of the Son alight on them collectively, a reaction of such intense beauty takes place that it transforms the surrounding landscape. But the reaction is not just beautiful; it is also powerful.

The many "atoms" that make up the local church, among which are husbands and wives for whom the local church has become a base of operations, begin to pass back and forth expressions of the love of Christ. This produces in turn multiple reactions, explosive reactions, filling the church with a surplus of love, spilling out onto other members of the family of Christ, causing another series of reactions to take place—each one reverberating with cruciform love and together producing a magnificent portrait.

Soon, someone whose trek through life has stumbled against one obstacle too many, whose path is littered with deadfall and decomposition, whose feet are caught in quagmires of disappointment and despair, whose heart is desperate for any kind of release—soon this someone will stumble upon the love of Christ reverberating within the local church and will raise a cry to other weary travelers in the expedition of life: "Here at last is what I have been looking for! Here is salvation!"

Oh to be models of that portrait! Oh to be lights to a dark world! Oh to be husbands and wives enmeshed in the local church!

10

NEITHER ODDS NOR ENDS

I have known many happy marriages, but never a compatible one.
. . . For a man and a woman, as such, are incompatible.

G. K. CHESTERTON

Marriage is like a volcano. When peaceful, it can be one of the most pleasing sights of creation. But when eruptions begin, it can turn ugly very quickly. In marriage, most eruptions spew only a bit of steam and generate only a few tremors. Sometimes, however, they churn out molten heat day after day. Occasionally they blow the tops off marriages and turn what were once promising unions into empty craters. Such eruptions nearly always arrive by stealth; friction begins long before partners are aware of it. It is important to detect the early signs of this friction and to administer the only sure corrective—the glory of God in the cruciform love of Jesus Christ.

FEAR

Fear can be the most insidious eruption within marriage, and not just fear of circumstances—the impending loss of a job or the chronic illness of a child—but fear of one's partner. Rarely are husbands and wives aware of this fear, even though it may have been brewing for years. Over time, a wife's fear of her husband may grow in several directions. She may fear his unsympathetic heart, his uncompromising spirit, his rigid opinions, his pessimistic responses, his stinging rebukes, his volatile anger, his depressive moods, his incessant laziness, his stony silence, his threat of abandonment. Similarly, a husband may subconsciously fear his wife. He may fear her independent spirit, her nagging tone, her lack of respect, her caustic rebuffs, her sexual disinterest, her stoic indifference, her idealistic expectations, her persistent whining, her fickle emotions.

Fears like these can undermine a relationship, especially when partners begin to anticipate negative patterns in the other, imagining the worst and dreading the inevitable. At this point, the pressure arrow quivers in the red zone, and emotions can flare up dangerously—all because of fear.

It is vital to understand the anatomy of fear. At root, fear derives from a sense of powerlessness—the inability to control a partner according to one's wishes. When fear is awakened, it inevitably begets even deeper fears as partners become increasingly frustrated over their powerlessness to shape the other.

Fear, however, can be beneficial. It can highlight a vital truth: we are not all-powerful. This can in turn drive us into the arms of the omnipotent One. It can awaken trust in Jesus Christ. And when it does, when by faith we submit ourselves to the sovereign care of the Lord's rule over our lives, we are candidates for transformation into his image and for reproduction of his love. That is the positive outcome of our fears. And his love will not seek to change a partner according to one's own wishes but rather to serve a partner. And when a partnership is marked by loving service, fears begin to subside.

Three wives were once married to difficult husbands. One of the husbands was introspective and a workaholic, another was impulsive and sarcastic, and the last was emotional and restless. Each of the husbands suffered from debilitating bouts of depression. All three gave their wives reason to fear. Yet when the husbands died, each of the wives composed a heartfelt tribute. From Sarah Edwards after the passing of Jonathan came gratitude: "What shall I say? A holy and good God has covered us with a dark cloud. . . . [But the Lord] has made me adore his goodness, that we had him so long. . . . Oh what a legacy my husband . . . has left us!"[1] From Katherine Luther after the homegoing of Martin: "If I had a principality or an empire and lost it, it would not be as painful as it is now that the dear Lord God has taken from me this precious and beloved man."[2] And finally from Susannah Spurgeon after the death of Charles: "Now that I am parted from thee, not for a few days only . . . but 'until the day break, and the shadows flee away,' I think I hear again thy loving voice saying, 'Don't cry over your lamb, wifey,' as I try to give thee up ungrudgingly to God—not without tears,—ah, no! that is not possible."[3]

Clearly, the three wives received more from their husbands than fear. They were the beneficiaries of a Christlike love that "covers a multitude of sins" (1 Pet. 4:8). In return the wives responded to the trials of their husbands, not by trying to change them but by serving them at their points of need. These two expressions of love, one from the husbands and one from the wives, served to dissipate fear because "there is no fear in love, but perfect love casts out fear" (1 John 4:18). When partners fill their marriages with expressions of selfless love, fears rarely trigger a full-scale eruption.

May we as husbands and wives be alert to our fears! And may our fears drive us to Christ! And may Christ fill us with love for one another! And may our love dissipate our fears!

WEAKNESSES

Everyone has a weakness, perhaps many weaknesses. And there is nothing like marriage to expose them. When two people live in close proximity, they become acutely aware of the shortcomings of the other—the psychological flaws, the gnawing insecurities, the troubling obsessions, the lingering baggage, and the annoying quirks of personality. And weaknesses seldom go away; the faults of newlyweds usually persist into old age. When partners react to weaknesses with scorn, marriages languish. When they respond with grace, marriages blossom.

The weaknesses of marriage can usually be boiled down to two fundamental defects: the husband's failure to love his wife and the wife's failure to respect her husband (Eph. 5:33). Normally, we seek to resolve these deficiencies by encouraging each partner to work on his or her own defect, but this is not always the best approach. While it is true that partners ought to address their own weaknesses, it is equally true that they can assist in the overthrow of the weaknesses of the other.

Husbands can help their wives to overcome the weakness of withholding respect. How? By acting in ways worthy of their respect.

The best way to do this is to dignify a wife. The early church father John Chrysostom understood this well: "Show her that you set a high value on her company, that you desire nothing more than to be at home with her, far more than in the market-place. Put her before all your friends. Do not let love of your children eclipse your love of her. Pray with her. Go to church with her."[4] When wives are dignified in this way, they will respect their husbands.

Notice as well the advice of the seventeenth-century churchman Thomas Hooker: "The husband [should] tender his spouse with an indeared affection above all mortal creatures: This [should] appear by expressions of respect, [namely,] that all he hath is at her command, all he [does] is wholly for her contentment and comfort, and [all] his heart . . . runs with full tide and strength [into hers]."[5] When it becomes apparent to a wife that she forms the centerpiece of her husband's affections, the gift of respect will flow freely from her heart. When husbands take responsibility for the weaknesses of their wives, those weaknesses are replaced by strength.

Most wives want to respect their husbands. They want to do their husbands "good, and not harm, all the days of [their lives]" (Prov. 31:12). Too often husbands make it difficult for their wives to become the woman described in Proverbs 31. But they should make it easy. Beyond dignifying their wives, men should strive to present themselves as strong, confident, and courageous husbands, not as anxious, insecure, and defensive. Wives respond unwittingly to the demeanor of their husbands. When husbands are overcome by worry, wives may feel insecure. The trial of living with troubled husbands breeds disrespect.

How can a man be consistently more confident? It will not be by seeking to grow in self-confidence but by placing his confidence in the Lord (Josh. 1:8–9). The Lord is worthy of a husband's confidence, since the Lord alone is sovereign and able to work all things for his glory and the good of the husband (Rom. 8:28). When a woman sees her husband trusting in the Lord, she grows in her respect for her husband. Confident in the Lord, a husband turns a wife's weakness to strength. Husbands love their wives best when they help wives to respect them most.

Wives can also help their husbands to overcome the weakness of withholding their love. They can strive to be the sort of partner who elicits that love. Martin Luther describes such a wife: she "glows like a fire and desires nothing but the husband. She says, 'It is you I want, not what is yours: I want neither your silver nor your gold. I want only you. I want you in your entirety, or not at all.'"[6] By convincing husbands of their devotion, wives can overturn a weakness. They can help their husbands to pour out the gift of love. Wives respect their husbands most when they enable husbands to love them best.

It is remarkable what happens in a partnership when both husbands and wives minister to each other at the points of their weakness. When a husband encourages the respect of his wife by dignifying her and by placing his confidence in the Lord and when a wife encourages the love of her husband by devoting herself to him, two things happen. First of all, both partners, each taking ownership of the other's responsibility, begin to forget about secondary weaknesses like personality quirks or irritating habits; and, secondly, both partners are now so committed to helping with the other's responsibility that the principal weaknesses of marriage, the absence of love and respect, begin to fade away. Thus by helping each other with primary weaknesses, subsidiary weaknesses become inconsequential. Selfless love transforms marriage into something both strong and peaceful.

The key is, of course, to focus on the partner and not on oneself, encouraging the partner to express his love or her respect. This sort of other-directed focus is possible only when the love of Christ invades a union. May we implore the Lord to transform our hearts according to his image, making us full of his glory in the shape of cruciform love.

FORGIVENESS

Whenever one person offends another, an opportunity for forgiveness is created. Without forgiveness, wounds fester and mistrust increases. Nowhere is forgiveness more essential than in marriage. Husbands and wives share a very small patch of turf, and their nearness to each other only magnifies personal offenses. The number of offenses capable of erupting within marriage is endless: rudeness, insensitivity, unkindness, anger, exploitation, dishonesty, abuse, infidelity, betrayal, thoughtlessness, coarseness, neglect, harshness, insincerity, deception, addiction, aloofness, violence, indifference–to name only a few. When sins such as these are not smothered by forgiveness, they smolder and relationships suffer. Long ago Mark Twain reflected–tongue-in-cheek–on the incipient nature of marital sins: "A woman springs a sudden reproach upon [a man] which provokes a hot retort–and then she will presently ask [the man] to apologize."[7]

Finding comic relief amid personal offenses can sometimes diffuse the pain, as can acknowledging the inevitability of relational strife. The Puritan John Oxenbridge encouraged husbands and wives "[to limit] the expectation" and to remember they are marrying a child of Adam.[8] Similarly, Martin Luther cautioned: "It is impossible to keep peace between man and woman if they will not overlook each other's faults but watch everything to the smallest point; for who does not at times offend?–very many things must be ignored so that a peaceful relation may exist."[9]

But the hurt often runs so deep it is too difficult to overlook. The result: marital breakdown. Here is where forgiveness can mend a ruptured relationship–and not just when forgiveness is requested by the offending party but also when it is not requested at all.

Put succinctly, forgiveness is an act of unconditional grace. It is a gift given by the aggrieved party and consists of three elements: dropping all charges against the offender, asking for no compensation (either emotionally or materially), and bearing up the penalty for the wrong. In the case of marital infidelity, for instance, the one who forgives will drop the case against the one who was faithless and will personally absorb the cost (the grief and the suffering) of the unfaithful deed. That is forgiveness, radical forgiveness. Forgiveness is always radical.

At times, forgiveness may seem too radical to countenance,

especially in the face of chronic offenses. Yet without forgiveness, broken relationships cannot be mended. No restitution can earn forgiveness; it must be granted unconditionally. Making an offer of unconditional forgiveness is not only difficult, it is impossible. It requires a supernatural work of God implanting a spirit of forgiveness in the heart. Only the Lord can transform self-protective hearts into self-giving hearts, the sort of hearts required for forgiveness. We derive our ability to forgive from the Lord.

Such forgiveness was typical of Jesus, who on the cross responded to the crimes of his tormentors: "Father, forgive them, for they know not what they do" (Luke 23:34). This sort of cruciform love brings glory to God and repairs broken relationships, preventing simmering eruptions from blowing the tops off marriages.

When personal grievances fester in a marriage, we must turn to the Lord and ask for grace, pleading with him for the soft heart that enables us to forgive our partner. We must not underestimate the capacity of forgiveness to revive a human relationship. Forgiveness can lift a relationship to heights it would never have reached otherwise. Forgiveness is the healing balm of marriage.

DEATH

The final eruption is death. While acknowledging our mortality in traditional wedding vows—"till death do us part"—we seldom think of the prospect of death. Little is more painful than separation from our helper. Apart from losing a child, what could be more heartrending than saying goodbye to the one constant of our existence, the companion of our journey, the love of our life, the one who knows us better than anyone else and yet loves us anyway? To neglect the subject of death, especially in marriage, is a mistake.

Death always arrives prematurely. A walk through old cemeteries provides a sobering reminder of how many marriages were terminated in the early flushes of love, when husbands would gaze endearingly into the eyes of their expectant wives only to see those eyes forever closed by the travails of childbirth.

It happened to our twenty-sixth president, Theodore Roosevelt, who, when his proposal of marriage was accepted by a young woman named Alice, wrote in his diary: "The aim of my whole life shall be to make her happy, and to shield her and guard her from every trial; and, oh, how I shall cherish my sweet queen! How she, so pure and sweet and beautiful can think of marrying me I cannot understand, but I praise and thank God it is so."[10] Their love was snuffed out four years later when Alice died in her husband's arms while giving birth to their first child. Roosevelt's heart was so broken that he could never bring himself to speak her name again.

In an age of modern medicine, we can be grateful for the capacity to postpone death, but we cannot put it off indefinitely. But—and here is an important point—death does not have to be a baleful curse. In marriage, it can serve a positive good. The great eighteenth-century literary figure Samuel Johnson made the famous observation that nothing focuses the mind like an appointment with the gallows in the morning. We become different mentally in the face of imminent death.

When husbands and wives acknowledge their mortality openly and honestly, conceding that death could come in the morning, it softens their hearts, tenderizes their words, erases their bitternesses, eases their anger, enlarges their patience, prompts their forgiveness, sparks their affections, sharpens their attentiveness, sweetens their love—in a word, unifies their marriage.

It is a good idea for husbands and wives to walk among the gravestones of old cemeteries, if not literally, at least in their minds. It will cause them to talk together about death, about its potential nearness, and it will put eulogies in their mouths while they are still both alive. Husbands and wives ought to eulogize each other every day as though it may be their last day. Pity the partner who discovers only after the other dies a depth of love never fully expressed in life. Regrets can be devastating. On the other hand, knowing that expressions of love were frequently spoken brings peace to the heart in times of bereavement. Here is a noteworthy truth: expressions of love blossom most fully when people face the approach of their deaths most honestly.

But there is a more important reason why we ought to reckon honestly with the imminence of death. We live best when we are ready to die well. If we believe death terminates our existence, throwing us into a lifeless abyss, then we will live as though there were no tomorrow. As the old (especially Epicurean) philosophers maintained: "Let us eat and drink, for tomorrow we die" (see 1 Cor. 15:32). In other words, let us slake our thirst on temporal pleasures and give free reign to self-serving desires.

But if we believe that death represents a new beginning and that "he who raised the Lord Jesus will raise us also with Jesus" (2 Cor. 4:14) and that "whoever believes in [Jesus], though he die, yet shall he live" (John 1:25), then we will temper our pursuit of momentary gratifications, knowing that our real treasure is stored up in heaven, and we will throw ourselves into the service of the Lord and others. We will be free to live well. Those who know they will be raised one day with Christ are spurred on in the present to sacrificial service.

In the seventeenth century, Richard Baxter encouraged husbands and wives "to prepare each other for the approach of death, and to comfort each other in the hope of life eternal."[11] By this he meant more than drawing up wills and planning funerals. While it is certainly commendable to make arrangements for our departures, Baxter had something better in mind. "To prepare each other for the approach of death" means to "comfort each other in the hope of life eternal." Couples should remind each other that the greatest treasures are those of eternity "where neither moth nor rust destroys" (Matt. 6:20). To fret about the fleeting matters of earth is a waste of time. Instead, we must invest ourselves in legacies that last, the self-giving love that endures forever, and especially the sacrificial love of marriage.

In heaven, we will no longer marry and be given in marriage, but we most certainly will revel in a legacy of marital love. According to Spurgeon, the love of husbands and wives will flow "into an ocean of eternal felicity."[12] Husbands and wives who prepare each other for death elevate their marriages by pursuing the exalted purpose of laying up treasures in heaven.

DUTY

While still drawing insights from Baxter, it is worth noticing the practical ways partners can pour themselves into each other.

The common duty of the husband and the wife is:

Entirely to love each other;
and avoid all things that tend to quench your love.

To dwell together, and enjoy each other,
and faithfully join as helpers in the education of your children,
the government of the family,
and the management of your worldly business.

Especially to be helpers of each other's salvation:
to stir up each other to faith, love, and obedience, and good
        works:
to warn and help each other against sin, and all temptations;
to join in God's worship in the family, and in private:
to prepare each other for the approach of death,
and comfort each other in hopes of life eternal.

To avoid all dissensions, and to bear
with those infirmities in each other which you cannot cure:
to assuage, and not provoke, unruly passions;
and, in lawful things, to please each other.

To keep conjugal chastity and fidelity,
and to avoid all unseemly and immodest carriage with another,
which may stir up jealousy.

To help one another to bear each other's burdens
(and not by impatience to make them greater).
In poverty, crosses, sickness, dangers,
to comfort and support each other.
And to be delightful companions in holy love,
and heavenly hopes and duties, when all other comforts fail.[13]

REWARD

Today there is an urgent need to rediscover the remarkable plan of God for marriage. I say this not only because some marriages are mired in self-focus but also because of the great rewards of Christian marriage. It is worth repeating: marriage filled with the glory of God in the form of tangible expressions of Christ's love will become a beacon of light to a world desperately in need of such light. In addition, such a marriage will confer on its participants the great comforts of nurturing companionship, abiding joy, and eternal purpose.

What a joy to recapture this God-appointed and God-glorifying plan for marriage so that we can affirm with Luther the blessing of such a partnership: "Ah, dear God, marriage is not a thing of nature but a gift of God, the sweetest, the dearest, and the purest gift of life."[14]

11

SINGLE-HEARTEDNESS

I wish that all were as I myself am. But each has his own gift from God, one of one kind and one of another. To the unmarried and the widows I say that it is good for them to remain single as I am.

THE APOSTLE PAUL

This is a book about marriage—a subject of compelling interest to those who are unmarried. Not all singles entertain designs on marriage, but most are champions of strong marriages, acknowledging the vital role of marriage in the local church and in society at large.

But what role does an unmarried person play in the purposes of God? The answer is: an enormously strategic role!

A NEW TITLE FOR SINGLES

Before examining the biblical teaching on the role of singles, it is important first to register a slight unease with the very word *single*. It is an unfortunate term. It defines a person according to what he or she is not. To be single is to not be married, which implies marriage is the norm and singleness the exception. It is a negative way of categorizing a person. Who wants to be the exception? It would be much better to define unmarried people in a positive light, according to what they are.

In addition, the word *single* denotes isolation. According to the Oxford English Dictionary, to be *single* is to be "one by oneself," with an emphasis on "by oneself."[1] The word thus implies loneliness. Is it any wonder that single people sometimes wrestle with their identities, with their places in the mix of social relations, with their roles in the local church, when the word used to describe them marks them out as lonely and exceptions to the norm?

It will be encouraging to unmarried people to learn that the word *single* never appears in the Bible as a description of their status. In the quote at the top of the chapter taken from the apostle Paul in 1 Corinthians 7:7–8, the word *single* was actually *added* by the English translators. It does not appear in the Greek text.

It would be a worthy exercise to search for a new word—a positive, inclusive, and more edifying word—to define the identity of the unmarried person. On this matter, the apostle Paul provides lexical assistance. Whenever he uses the term *single*, he does so in reference to a relationship in which all people—single and married—can participate. And it is a relationship in which singles, especially, can flourish, precisely because they are single.

Consider 2 Corinthians 11:2–3: "I betrothed you to one husband, to present you as a pure virgin to Christ. But I am afraid that . . . your thoughts will be led astray from a sincere and pure devotion to Christ." This is a picture of spiritual marriage, the marriage of the church to Christ, a marriage in which all Christians participate, including those who are unmarried—children, widows, widowers, bachelorettes, bachelors, and those who have been divorced. For Paul, it is the most important marriage of all, and one we ought to view as our primary relationship.

The word *sincere*, here, is a beautiful term in the Greek, *haplotes*, which means literally "single-hearted." To be single-hearted is to be unmixed in devotion, having given oneself entirely to Christ "as a pure virgin," with a heart belonging exclusively to the Lord. The single-hearted person is married wholly to Christ, pursuing the will of Christ, obeying his counsel, investing in his work, drawing on his love, and living for his glory.

It is a role which unmarried people are ideally suited to play. Why? Because they are not burdened by the distractions of marriage and hence are better able to express single-hearted devotion to Christ.

The apostle Paul is very clear on this point:

> The unmarried man is anxious about the things of the Lord, how to please the Lord. But the married man is anxious about

worldly things, how to please his wife, *and his interests are divided.* And the unmarried or betrothed woman is anxious about the things of the Lord, how to be holy in body and spirit. But the married woman is anxious about worldly things, how to please her husband. I say this . . . to secure *your undivided devotion to the Lord.* (1 Cor. 7:32–35)

Few would disagree with this apostolic critique: marriage presents a bundle of distractions. Shortly after his wedding, Martin Luther sighed: "One wakes up in the morning and finds a pair of pigtails on the pillow which were not there before. . . . [Now] all my life is patience. I have to have patience with the pope, the heretics, my family, and Katie!"[2]

Single people possess a sizable advantage. Free from the distractions of marriage, they can pursue the work of Christ with single-hearted devotion; and to be undistracted in the most important work of all is to fulfill a very strategic role in the world. Here, then, is a positive title for those who are unmarried—no longer *single*, but *single-hearted.* It is a title to be relished.

In the early years of the nineteenth century, a young Cornish man by the name of Henry Martyn graduated top of his class in the University of Cambridge. His academic distinctions were sufficient to earn him a prestigious fellowship at St. John's College in Cambridge. But he declined the honor in order to become one of the first Christian missionaries to India. His pastor and mentor, the renowned preacher Charles Simeon, loved Martyn like a son and, even while supporting his missionary call, shed tears on the day his understudy sailed for India. It would be a final farewell for the two men, both single men and both single-hearted in their devotion to the work of Jesus Christ.

Once in India, Martyn worked assiduously on a Hindustani translation of the Bible, witnessed exactly one Christian convert during his sojourn on foreign soil, and contracted (probably) the plague, dying in Persia seven years after leaving England.

In 1812, a parcel arrived at Simeon's doorstep. It was a portrait of Martyn painted in India. "I could not bear to look upon it, but turned away, covering my face, and, in spite of every effort to the contrary, crying aloud with anguish," commented Simeon. The painting was placed over the fireplace in the dining room and Simeon was known to sigh to guests: "There, see that blessed man! What an expression of countenance! No one looks at me like he does; he never takes his eyes off me, and seems always to be saying, 'Be serious—be in earnest—don't trifle—don't trifle.'" Then Simeon would smile at the picture and add, "And I won't trifle—I won't trifle."[3]

Single-hearted people don't trifle. They know themselves to be enlisted in the most important work of all. They realize they are commissioned to direct the lost to a Savior. They stay focused. They love the gospel of Christ more than they love their own lives. And they are right to do so, for the gospel of Christ is the power of God to rescue this world from its misery and sin. Single-hearted people understand: undistracted by lesser things, they don't trifle.

If you are single—if you are single hearted!—relish your status. Don't grieve over the fact that you are unmarried, don't feel sorry for yourself, don't feel deprived, don't believe you have yet to find your place in life, don't work feverishly to find a mate, don't think that you occupy a lower rung among God's people, don't defer positions of leadership to those who are married. We should be exceedingly grateful that a bachelor named Paul never bemoaned his single status, to say nothing of the single Galilean named Jesus. Both used their singleness to great advantage. They threw themselves into the dawning kingdom of God with single-hearted devotion.

A PARENTAL ROLE FOR THE SINGLE-HEARTED

Even the lament that single people are denied the joy of bearing and raising children is not entirely accurate. It is certainly not a view shared by the apostle Paul. "Though you have countless guides in Christ, you do not have many fathers. For I became your father in Christ Jesus" (1 Cor. 4:15). This single apostle was involved in procreation of the most important kind, not the birth of natural children but of spiritual children, and not a mere quiver full but entire churches full of children reborn through his teaching. This kind of paternity is not simply accessible to the unmarried but especially accessible to the unmarried, since they can pursue the vocation of spiritual parenting with single-hearted devotion.

Here, then, is a prescription to cure the blues of any unmarried person: you can be a procreator in the family of God. You can lead people to Christ, nurture people in Christ, and commission people for Christ. May single-hearted people be satisfied with nothing less, since they could scarcely obtain more! What is more rewarding than becoming fathers to children reborn in Jesus Christ?

It is not just the role of a father that single-hearted people are equipped to perform, but also the role of a mother. Listen again to the apostle Paul: "We were gentle among you, like a nursing mother taking care of her own children. So, being affectionately desirous of you, we were ready to share with you not only the gospel of God but also our own selves, because you had become very dear to us" (1 Thess. 2:7–8). This is the extraordinary confession of a male apostle—he shares all the maternal instincts of a mother who lays down her life for her children.

As a single apostle, Paul is thus a father and a mother, and to a quantity of children far more numerous than what he could have produced as a natural parent, a family representing the largest gathering of siblings anywhere on the planet, the only family capable of leading the world out of its darkness and into the eternal light of heaven.

The role of singles in spiritual parenting—both mothering and fathering—is not an innovation of the apostle Paul. It is a vocation announced throughout the Scriptures. In the prophetic book of Isaiah, we read about the special blessing conferred on eunuchs, a class of men unable to father natural children:

> For thus says the LORD:
> "To the eunuchs who keep my Sabbaths,
> who choose the things that please me
> and hold fast my covenant,

I will give in my house and within my walls
   a monument and a name
   better than sons and daughters;
I will give them an everlasting name
   that shall not be cut off . . . .
   [namely,] foreigners who join themselves to the LORD,
   to minister to him, to love the name of the LORD,
   and to be his servants, . . .
   these I will bring to my holy mountain." (Isa. 56:4–7)

This is a remarkable promise. To those who do not marry and, therefore, who do not bear natural sons and daughters, a great blessing will be given: a monument within the walls of the house of the Lord and an everlasting name that shall never be cut off. What is the monument? What is the everlasting name? It is the scores of foreigners drawn into the house of the Lord and made recipients of the eternal covenant. How will these foreigners, these strangers to God, be introduced into the heavenly family? By ministering eunuchs, who are single-hearted in their devotion to the Lord, and who generate a progeny more numerous and everlasting than naturally bearing fathers.

If you are single—and everyone is single at one point or another—here is the critical question: Whom are you parenting? Where are your children? Which foreigners are you bringing into the family of God?

Happily, it is not a difficult task to bring in foreigners. The harvest, we are told, is plentiful (Luke 10:2). The fields are white for harvest (John 4:35). What is difficult is finding single-hearted people who are devoted to the task, eager to reap a harvest of souls, desperate for dying human beings to be given everlasting names. As a single person, you are more advantageously positioned for this strategic work than your married counterparts. Do you believe it? Are you bringing in the harvest?

MISSIONAL SINGLES

Recently, I had an interesting conversation on an airplane with a man who announced to me that he possessed the "anointing of the priesthood" in the Church of Jesus Christ of Latter Day Saints. It was a new concept to me, so I opened up my carry-on bag and pulled out a Bible to see whether the idea enjoyed the imprimatur of God, whereupon my traveling companion reached down into his even larger bag and pulled out two books, a Bible and the Book of Mormon.

Before long, he was passionately urging me to read the Book of Mormon cover to cover, which prompted me to ask a question that had long been percolating in my mind: "If you did not have the Book of Mormon, what would you lose?" Without hesitation and with tears welling up in his eyes, he replied, "I would lose the joy of knowing that my four sons, while still single, sacrificed themselves to two years of mission work, discovering the joy of evangelism. That is something you, without the Book of Mormon, don't have—fifty-three thousand single Mormon missionaries reaching six million people!"

My first thought was somewhat apologetic: "Perhaps you're right, we don't have that." But my second thought was more accurate: "You're wrong! It's a cardinal teaching of the Bible, in both Old and New Testaments, that single people can and do bear spiritual children."

It's a rich blessing to be single. It opens up doors often inaccessible to married people. Are the single-hearted walking through those doors?

Jesus himself, in his teaching on marriage, set out the advantages of being unmarried. "'A man shall leave his father and his mother and hold fast to his wife. . . . ' So, they are no longer two but one flesh. What therefore God has joined together, let not man separate" (Matt. 19:5–6). In other words, there is no way out for married people. Stunned by these words, the disciples exclaimed: "If such is the case of a man with his wife, it is better not to marry" (Matt. 19:10). To which Jesus responded: "[That's why] there are eunuchs . . . for the sake of the kingdom of heaven" (Matt. 19:12). That's why people remain unmarried, so that they may be free to serve without distraction in the kingdom of Christ.

If you are a Christian and not married, you are qualified for this exalted service. It is a thrilling calling.

EXAMPLES OF SINGLE-HEARTEDNESS

David Brainerd was single and single-hearted. He foreswore the comforts of early eighteenth-century New England for the trials of serving Indians on an inhospitable frontier. While the intelligentsia back home debated whether Native Americans were fully human, the young Brainerd worked earnestly for their conversion to Christ—and at great cost both to his reputation and ultimately to his health. He died of tuberculosis at the young age of twenty-nine, but not before he could praise God for a handful of conversions and could compose a diary which, when published later by Jonathan Edwards, helped to spawn the modern missionary movement. Several generations of missionaries have emerged from that movement, and many have trekked to the distant reaches of the globe with the same good news of Jesus Christ that Brainerd carried to the wilds of America. The work of the single-hearted Brainerd continues to this day, his sacrifice long ago still prompting the birth of yet more children who now possess names written in eternity.

Henrietta Mears was single and single-hearted. Some viewed her as frumpy—decked out in garish hats, exotic feathers streaming in every direction, sporting Coke-bottle-thick glasses, and walking with a pronounced lilt. She was, in her early sixties, a unique character, a bona fide spinster, but the young people loved her. They called her, reverently, "Teacher"—for who else could expound God's Word with such holy conviction as Miss Mears?

Through her teaching in the middle years of the last century, the work of Christ grew dramatically, with the emergence of the largest church-based college ministry in America, the production of a comprehensive Sunday school curriculum used by churches around the world, and the founding of a mountain retreat center called Forest Home, where thousands have entrusted their lives to Jesus Christ and where many others began their service of Christ. Some of the largest evangelical organizations in our world today were founded by people nurtured by Miss Mears. This amusing and wonderful woman, this single woman, this single-hearted woman, is even now, more than four decades after being called to the side of her Savior, bearing spiritual children for Christ.

By now it will be clear why Paul issues the exhortation: "To the unmarried and the widows I say that it is good for them to remain single as I am" (1 Cor. 7:8). How could a person trade such a strategic position for one prone to distraction? The tragedy is that many fail to appreciate the blessings of being single. Reading inspiring stories about Brainerd or Mears or about other fruitful singles leads readers to imagine that such people are the exception, not the norm. Not many possess the unshakable fortitude of Brainerd or the compelling teaching gift of Mears. True—in fact no one else does! Each was unique in his or her own way. But so is *every* unmarried person. Everyone is equipped with a special package of skills to be used wherever he or she has been placed by God—in a local church, in a specific neighborhood, in a particular school, in a downtown office.

If you are single, do not underestimate what God can do through you exactly as you are and where you are. You have been prepared by his sovereign will to shape the future of the world. Be alert to extraordinary possibilities of ministry. Anticipate the joy of being used by God to change the hearts of family, friends, and colleagues. Pray earnestly for this blessing. Live the undistracted life, prepared to minister in places of pain and darkness, giving witness to the gospel of Jesus Christ. Thank God for your singleness. Praise him for the gift of single-hearted devotion to the greatest work of all, the work of the kingdom of Christ.

FROM SINGLE TO MARRIED

Statistics do indicate, however, that most people nurture romantic aspirations. Is this a reality to be discouraged? No! Even the apostle Paul, who is at pains to promote the advantages of the single life, refuses to stand in the way of those who desire to be married. Nor does a once-celibate monk named Luther, who argues that singles-for-life "are rare, not one in a thousand, and special miracles of God."

While this is doubtless an instance of hyperbole, there is no mistaking the popular appeal of marriage. It is thus vital, especially in a chapter devoted to singleness, to consider what the Bible has to say about looking for a mate. How should an unmarried person who wants to be married proceed in search of a partner?

Seeking Christian Mates

The most important and nonnegotiable principle is to look for a person who shares a single-hearted devotion to Jesus Christ. This is the basis for a God-glorifying marriage. Two become one flesh when they inundate each other with expressions of the love of Christ. But only those who are in Christ can express the love of Christ. So much depends, then, on marrying a person of single-hearted devotion to Christ.

In the classic allegory *Pilgrim's Progress*, a young woman by the name of Mercy is pursued by a man called Mr. Brisk. Mercy asks her friends about the suitability of this man's character. What she learns is disconcerting: he is "a very busy young man . . . that pretended to religion" but is probably "a stranger to the power of that which was good." The report settles the matter for Mercy: "Nay then, I will look no more on him, for I purpose never to have a clog to my soul."[4]

The precise nature of this "clog" is spelled out by Richard Baxter, a Puritan pastor from the 1600s: "If you should marry one who proves ungodly, how exceedingly great the affliction will be! If you love him [or her], your soul will be in continual danger; he [or she] will be the most powerful instrument in the world to pervert your thinking, deaden your heart, take you off from a holy life, kill your prayers, and corrupt your life."[5] These are strong words and probably sound overblown to modern ears, but who would want to venture a relationship with one who might "deaden" one's most precious possession, a heart alive to the Lord?

The counsel of the Bible is even more direct. Several times in the Old Testament the people of God are warned against marrying unbelievers. "You shall not enter into marriage with [foreigners], neither shall they with you, for surely they will turn away your heart after their gods" (1 Kings 11:2; see also Ex. 34:12–17; Ezra 10:1–17; Mal. 2:11). It might be wondered, how could an unbeliever ever disrupt a believer's devotion to the Lord? It does not take much. The great and the wise King Solomon, when old, confessed that "his heart was not *wholly* true to the LORD" (1 Kings 11:4), a malady attributed to his mixed marriages. He had yoked himself to unbelievers and lost his spiritual edge. He no longer exhibited single-hearted devotion to the Lord. Such devotion is too precious to subject to even the slightest risk.

The partner who is destined to become your closest friend, your most trusted confidant, and your intimate lover will assuredly exert a great power over your heart. He or she will influence you in one of two directions: either drawing you closer to the Lord or pushing you away. For the glory of God, resist anyone who might lure you away. Above all, trust the Lord to lead you to a mate who will fortify your single-hearted devotion to Christ. "It is," says Baxter, "a mercy to have . . . a helper . . . to stir up in you the grace of God."[6]

Another Puritan, Daniel Rogers, who possessed a sensitive mind on matters of marriage, makes the following observation: "Marriage love is a secret work of God . . . who pitches the heart of one party upon another . . . a match therefore made in heaven . . . brought together by God . . . bred under one constellation, tempered by the influence of heaven. . . . Mercy and providence make [a couple] who say, 'See, God has determined us out of this vast world each for the other.'"[7]

Too often people grow impatient while waiting for a marital partner. Yet it is worth waiting for a match chiseled by "mercy and providence." Never rush into a relationship not "tempered by the influence of heaven." "Be not too hasty," says Baxter, "in your choice, but deliberate well, and thoroughly know the person on whom so much of the comfort or sorrow of your life will necessarily depend. . . . No care and caution can be too great in a matter of so great importance."[8]

It is possible of course to be too cautious in the evaluation of a mate and to become mired in overanalysis. How does one strike a balance between due diligence and excessive introspection? Several signposts point the way forward. First of all, seek to identify what God is doing in a relationship. Musing over a mate is a time for looking to God. He is sovereign over your life, and especially over the events that bring you into contact with a future partner. Always ask: Does the Lord appear to be involved in this relationship? Is there clear evidence of his hand at work in this budding romance? Is he giving the two of us together a desire to live for his glory? Are we united in single-hearted devotion to Jesus Christ? Is the Lord drawing us together in the miracle of one flesh?

Seeking Internal Beauty

Then, secondly, ask honestly: What is it that ultimately attracts me to this particular individual? Is it external features or internal qualities? Disposition of heart is more important than all external allurements put together. Chrysostom encourages us to look inside a person: "Seek out *soul* beauty. . . . External attractiveness . . . lasts only one or two months, or perhaps at most a year. What then? The level of admiration fades with familiarity. . . . In one who has *soul* beauty, the attractiveness does not fade . . . and continues ardent."[9] While not dismissing the importance of physical attraction (after all, the Lord did give us eyes to enjoy his handiwork!), it is more important to assess a person at the core of his or her being.

There is always the likelihood that some inner traits will remain undetected and emerge only later in marriage. And if those traits are disappointing, what does a person do then? He or she will trust the Lord for the ability to respond to those traits lovingly, not critically.

Seeking Godly Counsel

Thirdly, it is crucial to seek the counsel of godly people. The old adage "love is blind" is a reminder that minds can become clouded by emotion. And since little is more emotional than romance, clear-mindedness can vanish very quickly. Thus it is prudent to draw on the unglazed perspective of others, especially those capable of detecting authentic devotion to Christ. The sixteenth-century Reformer Martin Bucer supports this advice: "One acts impiously if he [or she] enters the marriage contract, that lasting and highest union of human nature, without the counsel of important and pious people through whom he [or she] may be able to know the mind and the will of God with more certainty."[10]

Never fear the counsel of Christian confidants, especially when offered by those who know and love you most. Instead, seek it earnestly. Then take what is offered to the Lord in prayer.

Relinquishing Singleness Cautiously

Finally, do not relinquish your singleness too readily. Remember it is a gift from God. Consider the words of Baxter: "Oh that single persons . . . knew the preciousness of their leisure, and how free they are to attend the service of God, and learn his word, in comparison to the married!"[11]

Despite these encouraging words, many may still wonder how singleness can possibly compare to the delights of marriage and especially to the biblical ideal of marriage set out in this book. How can a single person enjoy the divine glory which irradiates between two partners who are bound together by mutual expressions of cruciform love?

The answer is that such glory lies within the grasp of all people, singles alike. Any person in whom Christ dwells, single or married, is able to replicate the biblical ideal of sacrificial love in relationships with others. The only difference is that a married person will probably bond more deeply with one person, while the single person will probably bond more broadly with many.

Thank God for the gift of singleness. It is not to be relinquished lightly.

12

CONCLUSION

AN INTENSIFYING GLORY

Give my kindest love to my dear wife, and tell her, that the uncommon union, which has so long subsisted between us, has been of such a nature, as I trust is spiritual, and therefore will continue forever.

JONATHAN EDWARDS

The words above were dictated by Jonathan Edwards in 1758 to his daughter Lucy in the waning hours of his life. He and his family had recently submitted to the smallpox inoculation, a precautionary measure against a disease prevalent in the environs of New Jersey, where he had accepted the presidency of what later would become Princeton University. While the children recovered without incident, he contracted a full-blown case of the disease, with poxes boiling up on the roof of his mouth and precluding the ingestion of liquids.

With fever wracking his already feeble frame, he called for Lucy and made the famous dictation. His thoughts settled immediately on his wife, Sarah, far away at their home in Stockbridge, herself struggling with illness. The phrase Edwards used to distill the essence of their marriage is one of the most beautiful ever to fall from human lips: "uncommon union."

A skeptic may wonder how a nondescript expression like "uncommon union" could possibly warrant such a generous accolade. Surely other terms, particularly those highlighted throughout the course of our study, deserve greater approbation—terms like "the glory of God," "the cross of Christ," "self-emptying love." These are the likely candidates for the most beautiful expression ever to grace the written page. Except for one factor—each of these allegedly superior phrases is contained within the term "uncommon union."

THE GLORY OF CHRISTIAN MARRIAGE

Let us retrace our steps. Marriage is uncommon not because it is rare, but because it is distinct. It is unlike anything else in creation. It surpasses the most beautiful sight in nature. It occupies a strategic niche of society. It can change everything it brushes against into something better and brighter. Why? Because it is a repository of the weightiest commodity in the universe: the glory of God.

The marital bond was created to pulsate with divine glory—not a virtual glory, not a facsimile of the real thing, but the actual glory of God. When people see a Christian marriage, they ought to be overwhelmed by the incandescent splendor of God himself. It is truly an uncommon sight. But how can such a simple human relationship, a marriage between a man and a woman, possibly contain the wonder and the weight of divine glory?

It becomes possible when two people manifest together the image of Jesus Christ and especially the image of his cross. The glory of God never shone as brightly as it did on the broken face of Jesus, effervescing in the cruciform love of the Savior. It is an expression of the love of the Godhead, a love passed back and forth among Father, Son, and Holy Spirit from before the beginning of time, cementing a triunion of unspeakable wonder. When we, in conformity with the crucified Christ, image within our marriages the miracle of intertrinitarian love, a union of supernatural beauty takes shape—an uncommon union, a union radiating with the glory of God in the shape of cruciform love.

CHRIST-CENTEREDNESS

The key is the crucified Christ. Most of the time we think about the cross in terms of its work in our initial salvation (since through the death of Christ we receive the gifts of justification and regeneration), and too seldom do we think about the cross in terms of its ongoing work in our lives. The implications of the cross for our daily existence are immense. Husbands and wives who fix their eyes on the cross, beholding its glory, are transformed into the very same image, exhibiting its sacrificial love and reflecting increasing incre- ments of its glory (2 Cor. 3:18).

How do we actually fix our eyes on the glory of the Lord? The answer is simple: by looking for it in the book where it is featured most prominently, in our Bibles. The glory of God is emblazoned on page after page. We must take up the pickax and dig deeply into God's Word. We must work a profitable quarry—such as an espe- cially glory-saturated paragraph—over and over. We must pray for deeper strikes of glory, yearn for richer veins of meaning, seeking greater insight into the work of the crucified and risen Jesus.

The more we look at the glory of the Lord, and especially the more we look at the treasure of his cross—where all the brightness of divine love devolves onto one stricken head—the more we will come to resemble the object of our focus, and hence the more the love of Jesus will inundate our marriages, transforming them into unions of profound beauty, uncommon unions, indissoluble unions, unions cemented by the firm epoxy of Christ's love.

We can see now why the glory of the Lord is to be viewed as the irreplaceable tether that binds a marriage and propels two people to ever greater heights and more majestic peaks.

PUTTING ON CHRIST

If the call to fix our eyes on the glory of the Lord in the pages of Scripture is of practical help to our marriages, a second insight may prove even more beneficial. In the epistle to the Romans, the apostle Paul issues a strong exhortation: "Put on the Lord Jesus Christ, and make no provision for the flesh" (Rom. 13:14). This may well be the most important piece of marital advice ever written.

It is immediately clear that Paul is using a metaphor drawn from the fashion-conscious world of the first century. Clothing, it was held back then, shaped a person's identity. By encouraging his readers to "put on the Lord Jesus Christ" just as they would put on an article of clothing, Paul is urging them to find their identity in Christ. When husbands and wives accept this apostolic challenge and cloak themselves with the Lord Jesus Christ, draping themselves in his self-giving love, they will be poised to step onto the runway of marital glory.

Dispensing with Sin

But exactly how do we put on the Lord Jesus Christ? First of all, we must take off the old attire and throw it into the dustbin. Husbands and wives must strip off old garments—in particular, according to Paul, they must make "no provision for the flesh."

The flesh is a despicable piece of clothing. It is stained irreversibly with selfishness and sin and when it is allowed to shape the identities of two people in marriage, it invariably drives them apart. In fact, most problems in marriage can be traced to this one mangled piece of clothing: the self-besotted flesh.

Husbands and wives must acknowledge the wretched condition of the old garment and confess to being cloaked head to toe in the selfishness of its frayed threads. It is a painful confession: few of us are eager to own our self-centeredness. Yet nothing could be more obvious to two parties in marriage, where the barbs of self intrude with alarming frequency. It is a good confession to make. Before we can put on the Lord Jesus Christ, we must come to acknowledge and to loathe our old attire.

Pleading for Help

Secondly, we must admit that, however much we dislike our old rags, we are helpless to strip them away. Selfishness is a garment not only glued to our bodies but also manacled to our souls. It will require more than willpower to banish the flesh—more than new resolve, more than trying harder, more than marital counseling, more than the next innovative book on relationships, more than anything mere human beings can bring to the table. If the blot of selfishness is to be stricken from our marriages, we will need assistance of a supernatural kind. To make "no provision for the flesh" we will need to look for help outside ourselves.

Precisely! In every good marriage, there will be a double dose of humility: an acknowledgement of the blight of selfishness and an admission of inability to do anything about it. Then and only then will two people be ready to put on the Lord Jesus Christ, because then and only then will they raise an ardent plea to the Lord, asking him to do in their marriage what they cannot do for themselves: remove the ragged garment of selfishness and replace it with a suit of selflessness.

Identifying with Christ

Thirdly, we may now venture to put on the Lord Jesus Christ. It may sound like a taxing endeavor, but it is actually quite straightforward. Just as we have been unable by ourselves to remove the garment of selfishness, so we are incapable of cloaking ourselves with Christ. But praise God—both the stripping off and the putting on are gifts of his grace.

What does it mean to put on the Lord Jesus Christ? It means to rehearse over and over what the Lord Jesus Christ has already accomplished on our behalf and how those accomplishments, especially those of the cross and the resurrection, *shape our identity completely*. In the case of husbands and wives, it means to recognize that the Lord has "condemned sin in the flesh" (Rom. 8:3) and that we no longer need to wear the rags of selfishness. We have a new identity. We can cast off self-seeking behavior precisely because it was trampled underfoot by Christ. To put on the Lord Jesus Christ means to entrust ourselves to what he has accomplished in and for those who identify with him.

Husbands and wives . . . we must remind each other with regularity of the priceless identity we share in Christ. He has imprinted our very souls with the self-emptying love of his cross. He has filled us with the sin-defeating power of his resurrection. We have been impregnated, as it were, with all the fullness of the Godhead. We could not be more loved or more blessed.

Tragically, too many of us are unaware of the scope of this blessing. Too many husbands and wives do not know that they no longer need to descend into petty squabbles, bruised feelings, and stony silence. They are senseless to their identity in Christ. Here is a magnificent truth: as people in Christ we are no longer bound to be self-centered but are set free to be like Jesus.

That does not mean our marriages will automatically achieve perfection. They will not—not on this side of eternity. But until the day heaven dawns, we can pursue the blessing of entrusting our lives to Christ, lifting our prayers to him, and crying out for the grace to overcome selfishness and to model his self-giving love.

Husbands and wives . . . are we lifting our combined voices with this petition? Are we making it our prayer? Are we crying out to God, asking him to help us to "put on the Lord Jesus Christ, and make no provision for the flesh" (Rom. 13:14), asking him to help us to acknowledge that the pattern and power of Christ already dwell within us, asking him to help us to live in anticipation of an ongoing series of miracles in which our marital interactions come ever more closely to resemble the glory of God in the face of Jesus Christ?

Worshipping the Lord

Fourthly, when husbands and wives see evidence of the supernatural work of God in their marriages, they will respond with joyful thanksgiving. Nothing so unites a marriage as mutual worship of the Lord God Almighty. Happy is the couple who can identify in each other instances of spiritual growth, where each can pinpoint to the other evidence of selfish rags tossed into the trash and the righteousness of Jesus Christ donned in their place. May we excel at encouraging one another in our marriages—confirming verbally to each other evidence of growth in Christ—and may we celebrate that growth by uniting together in thanksgiving to God for his gracious provision.

SUMMARY

The apostle Paul has just mapped out the trail to a God-glorifying marriage. It is a priceless trail. And its signposts bear repeating one last time. It begins with a problem, a big problem, and it's *our* problem. Every one of us, husbands and wives alike, is infected with self-centeredness; none of us naturally glorifies God. And it is a chronic problem. It won't go away. We are stuck, both victims and culprits in a thousand pitfalls and setbacks, and there is nothing we can do about it except to admit the problem. This is an absolutely critical step, indeed the decisive first step on the trail to a God-glorifying marriage.

The second step is humbly to look for help, to turn to the only One who can lift us out of the problem: Jesus Christ. On the cross, he dismantled the sin of our selfishness, bearing it away in his broken body and replacing it with the gift of his righteousness. He did this for God's glory and for the good of those who would by faith come to identify with him, who would venture their lives on the grace poured out on that cross. It is a grace that continues to affect our lives and especially our marriages.

Husbands and wives, we must remind each other of this work. The pattern of cruciform love has been stamped onto our very souls. The power of the resurrection continues to transform our lives. May we remember this! May we study this! May we cherish this! May it be our joy to put on the Lord Jesus Christ! Daily! Otherwise, we shall revert to negotiating the trail in our own ways and by our own strength, effectively returning to the dustbin and pulling out the old clothes. But with eyes fixed on Christ, we can model his love and draw on his strength and push on to the marital summit with thanksgiving in our hearts and rejoicing on our lips, all to the glory of God.

The trail features Jesus Christ at every turn. It runs through Christ, is negotiated in Christ, and is capped with Christ. The Lord Jesus Christ is the key to God-glorifying marriage.

Marital counsel that does not feature Christ, that does not seek to apply the work of his cross daily to the vicissitudes of marriage, will give couples perhaps interesting tidbits of advice that produce fleeting instances of encouragement but will leave them ultimately frustrated, stranded at hopelessly lower elevations. In Christ Jesus, we can climb so much higher.

Rummaging through my bed-stand recently, I came across a clutch of anniversary cards—carefully stowed and gratefully cherished—in which the words of my best friend and lover, the wife of my youth, Lesli, nurtured my heart once again with reminiscences of our years together. In one of those cards, its cover featuring a picture of a cute little girl playing at the sea, she writes:

> So this is what God had in mind for marriage. We've been to Paradise and Gethsemane, and to all places in between. We have confessed our weaknesses to God and to each other and he has confirmed, in a thousand ways never imagined, the beauty and the strength of our union. I am moved with eternal gratitude to God for meshing our lives as one in Christ. Upward we go, my Love, together for the Lord's glory!

Then, having dealt with important matters first, my wife, true to form, concludes with an unscientific postscript: "There is more this little girl wanted to say but I'll close by asking: 'Can you come out and play?'"

ADDENDUM

Several months have elapsed since I wrote the words on the prior pages, and during that time significant events have altered my life appreciably. After years of failing memory, my mom received a heavenward call, slipping away gracefully into the hands of a Savior she never forgot and adored to the last. Thus ended the earthly partnership of my parents, which for so long served as my template of a Christ-filled marriage.

Sifting through family papers, I discovered a poem written by my dad just hours before he, in 1951, took my mom's hand into his for better or for worse. As a dashing young businessman in Hollywood, Dad dated some of the rising starlets of the movie industry. When introduced to new life in Jesus Christ, he modified some of his romantic goals and began looking for a woman who would share his passion to live for Christ. The following verses chronicle that passion.

When Three Is Not A Crowd

> Years ago with confidence I'd engineer my date,
> Knowing just the type for me, I'd boldly chase a mate.
> Take advice from others? I'd protest strong and loud,
> "Two's pleasant company, but three's a noisy crowd."
>
> Then the Creator I did meet, and watched him plan
>   my life.
> Knowing if I'd trust in him, he'd surely find a wife.
> Guided by his perfect plan, to his good will I bowed,
> Suddenly it dawned on me that three is not a crowd!

So to a new and faithful Friend my needs I did confide,
Trusting with a humble heart, he was my sovereign guide.
Then came an answer–"Here she is!"–doubt vanished in a
     cloud,
Yes 'tis true, when Christ is there, that three is not a crowd.

Hand-in-hand we knelt as one with love that's oh-so-sweet,
With our two hearts outstretched to God, our union made
     complete.
And so with Christ's own love within, our hearts now full
     endowed,
Assured by his sustaining grace, that three is not a crowd.

Fifty-nine years later, after daily exchanges of the love of Christ, my parents' union was as sound as it was beautiful. Who can fathom the disorienting haze that must have engulfed my father when the union suddenly unraveled, when he was asked to bid farewell to his "love oh-so-sweet"?

R. S. Thomas, a vicar from rural Wales, puts the quandary of a bereft husband into words, shortly after losing his own wife of fifty years.

We met
under a shower
of bird-notes.
Fifty years passed,
love's moment
in a world in
servitude to time.
She was young;
I kissed with my eyes
closed and opened
them on her wrinkles.
"Come," said death,
choosing her as his
partner for
the last dance. And she,
who in life

had done everything
with a bird's grace,
opened her bill now
for the shedding
of one sigh no
heavier than a feather.[1]

For people who live "in a world in servitude to time," this poem pierces the vulnerable parts of the heart. But for my dad, who nurtures visions of eternity, who imagines my mom dancing in the presence of an eternal Savior, personal pain ushers his mind to heavenly realities and guides his pen in triumphant celebration.

My beloved now sees Jesus Christ face to face; and seeing him, she has become fully like him.

Those who knew her well will be hard pressed to imagine her more like Christ. In life she so clearly reflected the heart of our Lord, constantly giving herself in service to others. As the primary beneficiary of her love, I am both undone by her absence and buoyed by the assurance that she now has heard the Lord's commendation, "Well done, good and faithful servant, enter into the joy of your Lord."

What joy it must be! To see with no impairment the matchless beauty of Jesus Christ–I can only dimly imagine.

But . . . dimly no more. The breach of a lengthy marriage was temporary. Three-and-a-half months after releasing Mom into the eternal hands of Jesus Christ, Dad received his own heavenward call.

Now two people see fully, reflect Christ completely, and climb together for the glory of God.

NOTES

Prologue

1 D'Vera Cohn, Jeffrey Passel, Wendy Wong, and Gretchen Livingston, "Barely Half of U. S. Adults Are Married–A Record Low," Pew Research Center, accessed on January 9, 2012, http:// www.pewsocialtrends.org/2011/12/14/barely-half-of-u-s-adults-are-married-a-record-low/.

2 The study by psychologist and professor Cindy Hazan of Cornell University was reported by John Harlow in "True Love Is All Over in Thirty Months," *The Sunday Times*, July 25, 1999.

Chapter 1: Introduction: A Binding Glory

1 The assessment of David Olson, professor in the Department of Family Social Science at the University of Minnesota, as quoted by Michael J. McManus "Churches: Wedding Factories or Marriage Savers?" *National and International Religion Report* 7 (1993): 1.

2 Roland H. Bainton, *Here I Stand: A Life of Martin Luther* (Tring, England: Lion, 1978), 352.

Chapter 2: Something beyond Ourselves

1 "Climbing Mount Everest Is Work for Supermen," *New York Times*, March 18, 1923.

2 George Gallup Jr., in the foreword of a book by Michael J. McManus, *Marriage Savers: Helping Your Friends and Family Avoid Divorce* (Grand Rapids, MI: Zondervan, 1993), 11.

3 In Arnold Dallimore, *Spurgeon: A New Biography* (Edinburgh, UK: Banner of Truth, 1984), 61 (italics original).

4 In Ibid., 149.

Chapter 3: Cruciform Love

1 The observations of Armand M. Nicholi Jr., professor at Harvard Medical School and teaching psychiatrist in Massachusetts General Hospital, in a paper entitled, "What Do We Know About Successful Families?" (Plano, TX: Grad Resources Publishers, 1994).

Chapter 4: Transformation

1 Thomas Szasz, *The Second Sin* (New York: Anchor, 1973) 47.

2 Quoted by Charles Colson in "Living in the New Dark Ages," *Christianity Today*, October 20, 1989, 33.

3 Plato, *Timaeus,* trans. R. G. Bury (LCL, London: Heinemann, 1929), para. 91a, 249.

4 Aristotle, *On the Generation of Animals*, vol. 2, bk. 3, trans. A. L. Peck (LCL, London: Heinemann, 1943), 175.

5 Josephus, *Against Apion*, vol. 2, para. 201, trans. H. St. J. Thackeray (LCL, London: Heinemann, 1926), 373.

6 William Barclay, *Ephesians*. (Akron: St. Andrews, 1957), 199–200.

7 Mohandas Gandhi, *Gandhi: An Autobiography* (London: Jonathan Cape, 1949), 155.

8 *The Koran*, trans. N. J. Dawood (London: Penguin, 1956), 360–61.

9 John Stott, *Issues Facing Christians Today* (Basingstoke, UK: Marshall Morgan and Scott, 1984), 235–39.

Chapter 5: A Wife's Spirit

1 For the series of quotes see Roland H. Bainton, *Here I Stand: A Life of Martin Luther* (Tring, England: Lion, 1978), 288, 293, 302.

2 C. H. Spurgeon, *C. H. Spurgeon Autobiography Volume I: The Early Years 1834–1859*, compiled by Susannah Spurgeon and Joseph Harrald (Edinburgh, UK: Banner of Truth, 1962), 419.

3 Ibid., 410.

Chapter 6: A Husband's Love

1 Ecclesiasticus 25:26.

2 Jonathan Edwards, "On Sarah Pierpont," in *The Works of Jonathan Edwards*, ed. Perry Miller, John E. Smith, and Harry S. Stout, vol. 16 (New Haven, CT: Yale University Press, 1957), 789–90.

3 Sarah Edwards, to Esther Burr, April 3, 1758, George Claghorn transcription, in the Franklin Trask Library, Andover Newton Theological School, Newton Centre, Massachusetts; quoted in George M. Marsden, *Jonathan Edwards: A Life* (New Haven, CT: Yale University Press, 2003), 495.

Chapter 7: Becoming One Flesh

1 George Whitefield, *George Whitefield's Journals* (Edinburgh, UK: Banner of Truth, 1960), 476–77.

2 C. S. Lewis, *The Collected Letters of C. S. Lewis,* vol. 3, *Narnia, Cambridge, and Joy 1950–1963* (San Francisco: Harper, 2007), 8 November 1952.

Chapter 8: Fusing Bodies

1 Dio Chrysostom, *Discourses*, trans. J. W. Cohoon and H. Lamar Crosby (LCL, London: Heinemann, 1932), 37.34.

2 Malcolm Muggeridge, *Jesus Rediscovered* (New York: Doubleday, 1969), 78.

Chapter 9: In God's Church

1 C. H. Spurgeon, *C. H. Spurgeon Autobiography Volume I: The Early Years 1834–1859*, compiled by Susannah Spurgeon and Joseph Harrald, (Edinburgh, UK: Banner of Truth, 1962), 414.

Chapter 10: Neither Odds nor Ends

1 Sarah Edwards, to Esther Burr, April 3, 1758, George Claghorn transcription, in the Franklin Trask Library, Andover Newton Theological School, Newton Centre, Massachusetts; quoted in George M. Marsden, *Jonathan Edwards: A Life* (New Haven, CT: Yale University Press, 2003), 495.

2 Martin Marty, *Martin Luther: A Life* (London: Penguin, 2004), 188.

3 C. H. Spurgeon, *C. H. Spurgeon Autobiography Volume I: The Early Years 1834–1859*, compiled by Susannah Spurgeon and Joseph Harrald (Edinburgh, UK: Banner of Truth, 1962), 419.

4 John Chrysostam quoted in Thomas Oden, *Classical Pastoral Care IV: Crisis Ministries* (Grand Rapids, MI: Baker, 1994), 99.

5 J. I. Packer, *A Quest for Godliness: The Puritan Vision of the Christian Life* (Wheaton, IL: Crossway, 1990), 265.

6 Martin Luther quoted in Oden, *Classical Pastoral Care*, 100.

7 Mark Twain quoted in John Gross, *The Oxford Book of Aphorisms* (Oxford, England: Oxford University Press, 1983), 149.

8 John Oxenbridge quoted in Leland Ryken, *Worldly Saints: The Puritans as They Really Were* (Grand Rapids, MI: Zondervan, 1986), 51.

9 Martin Luther quoted in Oden, *Classical Pastoral Care*, 98.

10 Theodore Roosevelt quoted in Edmund Morris, *The Rise of Theodore Roosevelt* (New York: Random House, 1979), 102.

11 Richard Baxter, *The Practical Works of Richard Baxter*, vol. 1 (Sanford, FL: Soli Deo Gloria, 1990), 404.

12 Spurgeon, *C. H. Spurgeon Autobiography I*, 410.

13 Richard Baxter, *The Practical Works of the Rev. Richard Baxter IV* (Carlisle, PA: Paternoster, 1830), 234.

14 Martin Luther quoted in Roland Bainton, *What Christianity Says About Sex, Love and Marriage* (New York: Association, 1959), 82–83.

Chapter 11: Single-Heartedness

1 *Concise Oxford English Dictionary*, 11th ed., s.v. "single."

2 Martin Luther quoted in Roland Bainton, *Here I Stand: A Life of Martin Luther* (Tring, England: Lion, 1978), 290, 310.

3 Charles Simeon quoted in H. C. G. Moule, *Charles Simeon* (London: The Inter-Varsity Fellowship, 1892), 108.

4 John Bunyan, *The Pilgrim's Progress* (Harmondsworth, England: Penguin, 1965), 278–79.

5 Richard Baxter, *The Practical Works of Richard Baxter I* (Sanford, FL: Soli Deo Gloria, 1990), 400.

6 Richard Baxter quoted in Leland Ryken, *Worldly Saints: The Puritans as They Really Were* (Grand Rapids, MI: Zondervan, 1986), 43.

7 Daniel Rogers, *Matrimonial Honor* (Edification Press, 2010), 148.

8 Baxter, *Practical Works I*, 402.

9 John Chrysostam quoted in Thomas Oden, *Classical Pastoral Care IV: Crisis Ministries* (Grand Rapids, MI: Baker, 1994), 97.

10 Ibid., 98.

11 Baxter, *Practical Works I*, 399.

Addendum

1 R. S. Thomas, *Collected Poems: 1945–1990* (London: J. M. Dent, 1993).

GENERAL INDEX

SCRIPTURE INDEX

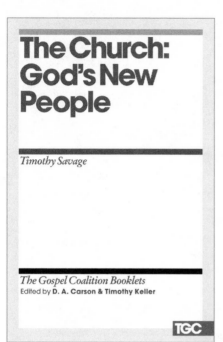

The Church:
God's New
People

Timothy Savage

The Gospel Coalition Booklets
Edited by **D. A. Carson & Timothy Keller**

TGC

A Gospel Coalition Booklet from Tim Savage

Author of *No Ordinary Marriage*

The church of Jesus Christ is the locus of God's plan for creation—
a plan to reclaim all things for his glory. In *The Church: God's New People*, Savage shows how it is within this corporate body that the larger dimensions of God's plan for creation receive breath-taking definition.